YOU

KISS

THE BRIDE

The Road Map—Choice, Engagement, Courtship, Marriage, Divorce, Remarriage, Polygamy...and the Christian

OKEY ONUZO

You May Kiss The Bride

All Bible quotations are from the King James Version except where otherwise stated.

ISBN: 978-1-880608-14-2
THIRD EDITION

Published by,
Life Link Worldwide Publishers,
175 Raymond Court Fayetteville GA.

For more information and book orders:
Visit: amazon.com

Email address: okeyonuzo@yahoo.co.uk

DEDICATION

To my family, my wife Mariam, our four children—Dilichi, Chinaza, Dinachi, Chibundu and all those who seek the will of God in marriage.

Whoso findeth a wife, findeth a good thing and obtaineth favour of the LORD. (Proverbs 18:22)

Marriage is honourable in all, and the bed undefiled: but whoremongers and adulterers God will judge. (Hebrews 13: 4)

All Bible quotations are from the King James Version except where otherwise stated.

ACKNOWLEDGMENTS

Thank you to everyone who has been part of this work, contributing in edits and reviews; Late Mrs. P. Ogundipe for a painstaking review work on the second edition and Nneka Okonkwo for sifting through the documents for areas for improvement on this third edition.

CONTENTS

PREFACE TO THIRD EDITION

You may kiss the bride." The order the couple waits for, a signal that the dream has become a reality. For some, it would be a long-awaited dream. It would also signal a real winding down from weeks and months of wedding preparations. "At last," they would say, "we are poised to begin to taste the pudding." The euphoria of the moment is often so immense as to block off any thoughts of life's realities and the challenges that lie ahead.

But then the day breaks, and the reality of being a spouse begins, and like novices, the couple begins to feel their way gingerly through the wilderness of married life. Indeed, "You May Kiss the Bride" is a signal that two have become one, that Adam and Eve have been recreated in two people, who have pledged to share their lives until death or Christ's return on earth, terminates the union.

While some remember the day, years later, with great nostalgia and realized dreams, others are not so fortunate. The realities of life have shattered some dreams as they remember the day with a whiff of bitterness when they recall the betrayal, the disappointment, and the disillusionment that had followed those noble dreams. They yearn for the love, the care, the tenderness, and concern embodied in that symbolic kiss before a crowd of witnesses.

Subsequent events in life have proven that some who pledged to share their lives till the end may not have done so with convictions deep enough to weather the storms of life. Some would honestly admit that what they felt initially could not have been love when judged by how they feel now. They are quite ready to accept fundamental incompatibilities that they now believe are irreconcilable differences.

The book, 'You May Kiss the Bride,' has come a long way from 1991 when it first appeared. Interest and comments have come from far and near, within and outside Nigeria. Comments centered around recognizing the cultural and religious diversity found among Christians and the Christian way of life. The controversies often center around the three critical questions of polygamy, divorce, and re-marriage. It has been a great challenge to find common grounds on these issues, given their accommodation in certain cultures and religions. Because there are peculiarities to some of the questions raised, we isolated their mention. The differences in opinions made it necessary to scrutinize the issues. The unanimity of view on each topic may be challenging to attain. What may be more achievable is the objective analysis of the guiding principles, which should leave the individual with the necessary information needed to make their own decision, guided hopefully by the law of the Spirit of life in Christ Jesus, and the state laws.

My prayer is that the Lord will use what is shared here to free those whose lives have been stagnated unnecessarily by apparent misconceptions while reigning in the consciences of those who may have mistaken our liberties in Christ for a license.

Other sections of the book have also been modified to accommodate new insights from God's Word, questions arising from technological developments in reproductive health, and principles from God's Word that help us navigate these developments.

You may indeed kiss your bride again and again. My prayer is that all couples who read this book live happily and in righteousness to fulfill God's purposes all the days of their lives. Every person, bachelor or spinster, desirous of a happy marriage finds marital peace and stability, in Jesus' precious name. Amen.

1

YOU MAY KISS THE BRIDE

The Vow

I, N, take You, M, to be my wedded wife, to have and to hold from this day forward, for better for worse, for richer for poorer, in sickness and in health, to love and to cherish, till death do us part, according to God's holy ordinance; and thereto I pledge thee my troth.

I, M, take You, N, to be my wedded husband, to have and to hold from this day forward, for better for worse, for richer for poorer, in sickness and in health, to love and to cherish, and to obey, till death do us part, according to God's holy ordinances; and thereto I give thee my troth.

For as much as N and M have consented together in holy wedlock, and have witnessed the same before God and this company and thereto have given and pledged their troth either to other, and have declared the same by giving and receiving of rings, and by joining of hands, I pronounce that they be husband and wife together, in the name of the Father, and of the Son, and the Holy Ghost. Amen.

"You may now kiss the bride."

Several years ago, I was at a wedding service in a particular Church in Benin City, Nigeria. Two friends of mine were getting married. It was a very lively service, and the Pastor, the officiating minister, was literally beside himself. He jumped and danced on the platform, and encouraged us, visitors, to exchange handkerchiefs with the "sisters," meaning the single ladies in his congregation if we liked them. It was quite interesting.

However, he advised the "sisters" to let him know of any and every proposal so he could scrutinize the young men to ensure that they were the right people. The ensuing drama was quite compelling. Hitherto. I was not aware that some churches exercised such detailed controls over their members' lives, concerning whom they should marry. I have since learned of similar monitored powers. I once heard of a young man whose strategy to escape the advice or an order by the church elders to part company with his fiancée could read like a thriller story.

That service proved memorable in more ways than one. The next most striking thing was the marriage vow. Hitherto, I had been used to hearing, "For better for worse, for richer for poorer, in sickness and in health, etc."

What the officiating minister read that day was entirely new to me: "For better and the best, for richer and the richest, in health, to love and to cherish, until we get to heaven... "I was not the only one surprised at this kind of "electrifying" set of vows. It was the subject of discussion that day, and for many days after, among us friends of the couple as we drove back to Ibadan (some two hundred and fifty kilometers from Benin).

Some felt that changing circumstances are a fact of life and that it was nothing short of psychological denial, if not downright self-deception, for anybody to make a vow like that. A vow is something binding that is supposed to have a guiding influence on conduct in life. The implication is that if anybody who has only vowed for better and the best encounters an adverse circumstance in his or her marital experience, then he or she may be justified to opt out since it was not supposed to be in the bargain.

Some of us felt that if a couple vows for richer and the richest, and for better and the best, it may be acceptable as a mind-set. It may just be an attitude adopted to cope with the vicissitudes or ups and downs of life, the existence of which are not denied. But there was a small minority who felt that for better and the best, and for richer and the richest was the ultimate expression of faith, designed to rule out all the negative elements of life and confess them out of existence, a view some of us considered quite simplistic.

Anyone who saw the original draft of the program I submitted to the vicar of St. Savior's Church, Lagos Island, Nigeria, where my wife and I wedded, would have noticed the ambivalence created by that Benin experience. "For better for worse," seemed to me like an expectation of adversities rather than a mere admission of reality. But I wasn't quite as bold as the officiating minister of that day in Benin. I modified our vows to read: not for better for worse, nor for richer for poorer: it was not for better and the best nor for richer and the richest either, but a somewhat beclouded, "Through every circumstance it may please the

Lord to let us pass through," which I felt left the reality of our ultimate experience firmly in God's hands, where I would prefer it to be.

When I took the draft to the vicar in-charge of our wedding venue, he almost flung it at me with these words; "What is all this rubbish? You cannot change the vows here. You must stick to the vows used by the Church, or you will not be allowed to use this Church," or words to that effect.

I had to delete my modification, hoping that the Lord would understand that the fault was that of the vicar from England and his conservative ways.

"For better for worse," which I ended up vowing, or "for better and the best" if you prefer it, hopefully as a mind-set only: either way, the problem of living in the will of God within marriage remains the same, from the moment you kiss the bride to signal the union.

You would have crossed many bridges of:

Choice: This means you must be fully persuaded of the person the Lord wants you to marry.

Connection: You must have met him or her.

Engagement: You must have engaged and courted.

Wedding: You must have planned and executed the wedding

It is only after all these that the journey will truly begin.

Whether you vowed "for better for worse," or "for better and the best," you will need the whole armor of God to keep winning all the way, and you will also need the whole armor of God to keep warding off adverse circumstances and situations.

The groom's symbolic kiss is to signal that the two parties have crossed the boundaries of choice, courtship, and wedding into marriage proper, where they will now grapple with the realities of life together as one.

Because of all the things that the Bible has to say about Christian marriage, many of which we shall deal with subsequently, it would be appropriate to say that a young man planting the symbolic kiss on his bride has led her beyond the point of no return.

As the vicar intones: "Wherefore what God has joined together, let not man put asunder," the couple must feel the union's finality come into place, like a curtain drawn to close the Act in a theatre.

Some vicars have taken the liberty to add, "What therefore God has joined together, let no man, let no woman, let no friend or brother or sister, or in-law or father or mother, and on and on to even circumstances of life, put asunder."

Because of this finality enshrined in the concept of Christian marriage, a discussion on it must move back to the place where the individual has to decide whom to marry. A great deal hinges on this, and on it hangs the question of stability or instability of the new home.

But is the decision that open-ended, or are there some guiding principles for the Christian?

And talking about stability within marriage, is this a by-product of chance or luck, or are there principles predictive by their nature? Is there a power to harness, someone to emulate, some transformation that we must experience to ensure stability as far as is humanly possible?

In other words, is there a veritable pathway to peace and stability within marriage, or must we all grope and hope that we stumble on the key or cord that assists a couple to vibrate in rhythm?

Stability in marriage will be an excellent place to start a discussion on marriage union, the conclusion of which is symbolized by the kissing of the bride.

Having examined the question of stability, we must consider the young men whose hearts are longing for the day they will be ordered by the priest to now kiss their bride and those young women who are longingly smoothening their cheeks to receive that kiss. It is after that that we shall survey the marriage proper and the many other questions that remain.

2

PATHWAY TO A STABLE MARRIAGE

In Proverbs 18:22, the Bible says, "Whoso findeth a wife findeth a good thing, and obtaineth favour from the Lord. But some people will say. "Yes, when we did find the wife, we were sure we found a good thing, but we don't know anymore."

Admittedly, there is a lot of chaos in the institution of marriage today. Many are facing pressure and choices that were unthinkable a few years back. Who could ever imagine homosexual and lesbian couples living an alternative lifestyle that the individual is free to choose? When you add the rate of abortion and divorce, the rise in single parenthood and sexually transmitted diseases, and the manipulation of genes, then we have the picture of an institution adrift in uncharted waters. Hedonistic ideas have set self-gratification at the pinnacle of human desire and effort.

The Bible, the final authority on principles that govern man's relationship with God, speaks about the divine purpose in the institution of marriage and outlines the path to stability and happiness.

Perspectives Of Stability

We will look at this subject from two angles because two major groups of people are searching for stability and happiness within marriage – THE SINGLES and THE MARRIED.

Some years ago, an elderly gentleman said: "Marriage is like a besieged city; those inside want to come out, and those outside want to go in." Perhaps, it is because of this that some prefer the halfway house where they are neither in nor out. They want to enjoy the benefits of married life by living together without its binding commitment and constraints.

There is no question that when two people from different backgrounds come together in marriage, blending into one family unit can be challenging. It is conceivably more so for those who cannot draw strength from God's Holy Spirit and who do not submit their lives to the authority of His Word, the Bible. Escape is often the only option that many see, and so they escape to wine, other women, other men, their job, their recreation, and some others to divorce. Nobody who has been through blending within marriage and has come out with a measure of success and happiness can ever say that it was easy. Nowhere is God's grace so much needed as in this process of integration. With a comic sense of resignation, a gentleman once told me that ever since God created the woman and gave her to man, neither God nor man nor his wife have rested.

There is a price to be paid for stability and happiness in marriage. Those who have achieved a measure of success are the envy of their peers. Everyone yearns for it. Thus, we should look at the fundamental principles that assist both the singles and the already married to achieve marriage stability.

The New Birth

The new birth is the beginning of the journey to character transformation. We come to Christ and accept Him as our personal Lord and Saviour. That singular act of faith means that we are now born again. But it is good to understand what transpired in the process. Let's take a look at John 1:12-13 (NKJV):

12 But as many as received Him, to them He gave the right to become children of God, to those who believe in His name:

13 who were born, not of blood, nor of the will of the flesh, nor of the will of man, but of God.

Those who give their lives to Christ are born of God. The most significant thing that transpired here is the indwelling presence of the Holy Spirit of God. Every believer in Christ should be aware that the Holy Spirit is given to us to be our teacher and guide. This truth we can see in John 14:26 (ISV)

26 But the Helper, the Holy Spirit, whom the Father will send in My name, will teach you all things and remind you of all that I have told you.

The other vital function is to bring us the mind of the all-knowing God, who sees the end from the beginning and everything in-between. This, too, we can see in 1 Corinthians 2:10-12 (ISV)

10 But God has revealed those things to us by his Spirit. For the Spirit searches everything, even the deep things of God.

11 Is there anyone who can understand his own thoughts except by his own inner spirit? In the same way, no one can know the thoughts of God except God's Spirit.

12 Now, we have not received the spirit of the world but the Spirit who comes from God, so that we can understand the things that were freely given to us by God.

The way to stability, love, and happiness in marriage is to invite God's Spirit to distill God's mind to empower us to conduct our affairs with godly wisdom. This is the practical essence of the new birth in Christ as stated in Romans 8:14 (ISV)

14 For all who are led by God's Spirit are God's children.

To be led by God's Spirit is to be in constant communion with the Spirit of God who can guide us and steer us as a couple to the path that leads to love, joy, and happiness within marriage.

The new birth has a practical and direct influence on joy and happiness within marriage. Two people bonded together within a family unit can follow godly principles in the Bible to discover that joy and happiness are not gifts but products of our choices; and hard work. If we make the right choices and respond correctly, we find lasting friendship, love, and joy. If we make the wrong choices and respond poorly, we reap what we sow as unhappiness and frustration.

Stability and the Communion of the Holy Spirit

When we seek guidance through the Holy Spirit, we admit that we do not have the wisdom to navigate the intricacies of blending two personalities from different backgrounds into one loving unit. The problem can be quite real. First, it is not often that we get married to someone we have known for a long time. When we court in a godly manner, we cannot see much of our potential mate as we have to always guard against the danger of immorality. Someone may say that we should still see enough of each other to detect traits that could lead to 'irreconcilable differences' in the future. And one can only say possibly!

It is possible to see things that may make us wonder if they are compatible with a happy union. The Holy Spirit will judge each streak of doubt and tell us whether they are significant or insignificant. For those just entering the marriage or about to do so, these reassurances assist us in no small measure to go confidently into the union.

The Spirit of God and the Choice

Life usually confronts us with many questions for which we need to make informed decisions. The handicap we have in making these decisions is our lack of complete knowledge of each situation's various factors, whether past, present, or future. For example, there is the all-important question about marriage for a man. Should I marry Miss A or Miss B? I recall the years before I finally proposed marriage to my wife when this question was before me as a dilemma. I vividly remember that the Spirit of God made it clear that there were those among my friends and acquaintances that I could relate to in marriage and those I could not. There were quite a few ladies who came my way and with whom I thought I had a reasonably good relationship that could blossom into a conceivably happy marriage given the right kind of stimulation. I recall times when I had put the question to the Lord in communion and had heard the Spirit of God say to me quite clearly: "That's not your type." That statement made me realize that it is not just everybody that one can marry within the worldwide community of Christians, as we would see later.

The issue of who is your type and who is not has a great deal to do with God's purposes for your life as one couple and your temperaments. Christian couples are to be traveling companions who journey to fulfill God's purposes for their lives together. But what exactly does this mean?

It means that the mate God will lead an individual to choose would be someone who would help him fulfill God's purposes for their life. There is a purpose for bringing together two people as husband and wife in the Lord, the pursuit of which should lead them to the highest degree of self-actualization and contentment.

Therefore, being born again is of very practical relevance to life in general and marriage in particular.

When we are led to choose someone as a partner in marriage, that is not to say that success is guaranteed. What it does mean is that they have the potential to succeed if they make the right choices and follow the correct principles. Time will tell whether the couple would achieve success or not. Relationships break down for many reasons. The fact of a break is not necessarily proof that the choice was wrong. Even the best pairing, as we shall see later, would still pose its challenges. Only those who live in obedience to God and His word can stand a good chance of success in their marriage. God can help us make the right choice. But we must go out there to prove that we believe it was the right choice for us by making it succeed. But more on this later.

Benefits Of The New Birth In Marriage

There is no intention here to look at this subject exhaustively. What is needed is to mention how the truths we imbibe as believers in Christ help us navigate married life.

God's Unchanging Nature

The first one is God's unchanging nature or His immutability. The prophet Malachi affirmed this in Malachi chapter 3, verse 6, which says: "For I am the Lord I change not; ..."

How does this have a bearing on marriage?

Born of God

A person born again is born of God, as the Bible explains in John chapter 1, verse 13. When we are born again, we have the potential to receive and manifest capacity beyond ability. This potential includes the capability to respond in love to one's spouse in any circumstance, which is well beyond any individual's natural ability. But the person who is born again or better still, born of God, learns to draw strength from God's supernatural ability through a process we may call the release of divine grace or divine enablement. The secret to this release of power is to consistently confess our weakness before Him when faced with life's challenges. His strength will then flow into us, granting us supernatural ability or what I call capacity beyond ability. He makes this strength readily available to those who have learned to trust Him.

Love for Life

When we are born again, we commit to obeying God and His Word. This commitment should change our mindset from worldly to godly. The godly perspective will accept the principles of holy living in the Bible and follow them wherever they apply. Here are two clear examples:

16 For the Lord, the God of Israel, says: I hate divorce and *marital separation and him who covers his garment [his wife] with violence. Therefore keep a watch upon your spirit [that it may be controlled by My Spirit], that you deal not treacherously* and *faithlessly [with your marriage mate].*
—Malachi 2:16 (AMP)

This Scripture speaks of divorce, physical abuse, and self-control. Because the LORD God Almighty hates divorce and physical abuse, we embrace self-control as a Fruit of the Spirit as we begin to contemplate marriage before entering the union. When you are praying for a marriage partner, you are thinking of a love for life, until death or rapture separate you.

Mind renewal is Mandatory.

There are many ungodly ideas that we need to scrap to develop a godly mindset. This change is fundamental to our Christian calling as seen in Romans 12:2 (AMP)

2 Do not be conformed to this world (this age), [fashioned after and adapted to its external, superficial customs], but be transformed (changed) by the [entire] renewal of your mind [by its new ideals and its new attitude], so that you may prove [for yourselves] what is the good and acceptable and perfect will of God, even the thing which is good and acceptable and perfect [in His sight for you].

Fruit of the Spirit

When we embrace Christ as Saviour, we allow the Holy Spirit within us to manifest His fruit through us. As a result, we equip ourselves with an armory of defense and survival tools to navigate the waters of post-marriage integration.

22 But the fruit of the [Holy] Spirit [the work which His presence within accomplishes] is love, joy (gladness), peace, patience (an even temper, forbearance), kindness, goodness (benevolence), faithfulness,

23 Gentleness (meekness, humility), self-control (self-restraint, continence). Against such things there is no law [that can bring a charge].

24 And those who belong to Christ Jesus (the Messiah) have crucified the flesh (the godless human nature) with its passions and appetites and desires.

25 If we live by the [Holy] Spirit, let us also walk by the Spirit. [If by the Holy Spirit we have our life in God, let us go forward walking in line, our conduct controlled by the Spirit.]

—*Galatians 5:22-25 (AMP)*

With these tools, love will cover many sins; joy will cause quarrels not to linger; inner peace will make us less reactive to provocation, and patience will send criticism and irritability to the cleaners. Goodness and kindness, which are friendship tools, will ensure that my spouse and I remain friends for life and correct each other in love. Faithfulness will keep us in each other's love and affection when we are together or away. Gentleness or meekness, which includes the virtue of humility, will ensure that we serve each other with joy. Self-control will ensure that we are never physically or verbally abusive but are temperate in all things.

Stability is a Choice

There are quite a few who may wonder why they have so much stress and strife in their relationship. The truth is that there is no mystery to this. Peace or strife are choices that we make daily. They are not about angels helping us or demons trying to pull us down. When we have misunderstanding or quarrel and choose to forgive each other, we have opted for the path of stability and peace. When we use our love to cover a multitude of wrongs, we are opting for stability. A lady once asked me: "*Is stability in marriage a matter of luck?*" My answer was no: Stability in marriage is a product of self-sacrificing love revealed in our daily choices. There is no magic or mystery to it.

The Help of the Holy Spirit

The greatest gift that our Lord Jesus Christ gave to His Church after He ascended to heaven was the Holy Spirit. He came to live in us to provide us with inner strength, counsel, and wisdom and correct us preemptively, so we don't look like fools through lack of discretion. His preemptive checks develop and mature us and cause us to manifest so much grace and virtue.

When we were newly married, my wife and I used to have quite a few arguments: eruptive and disruptive betimes. Then the Holy Spirit began to whisper to me during those exchanges: "*everything needful and useful that you need to say on this matter, you have said already. From now on, you say no more."* That was how the quarrels progressively died out. To lead a consistent Christian life is practically impossible without the Holy Spirit. Through the communion of the Holy Spirit, we learn to walk the path of stability in marriage.

Faith in God's Omnipotence

When the Bible repeatedly says that with God, nothing is impossible, those who have Him as their Father have great cause for joy if they can figure out how to tap into that source of power and provision. By trusting God and working out various biblical principles, a couple learns to trust God for many of their needs. As an undergraduate student at the University of Ibadan, I learned the truth of this Scripture firsthand:

Proverbs 11:24-25 (AMP)

24 There are those who [generously] scatter abroad, and yet increase more; there are those who withhold more than is fitting or what is justly due, but it results only in want.

25 The liberal person shall be enriched, and he who waters shall himself be watered.

I came to the university soon after the civil war ended, and because we lost the war, our financial state was very dire. But when I started giving to God's work and supporting Christian students in secondary schools that I visited, doors of opportunity opened to me to make income on the side as a student. After Part 1 MB, I was offered an academic exchange scholarship by the West German government under Willy Brandt to complete my medical education.

When we believe God's Word in the Bible and practice the principles it teaches, the omnipotent God opens doors of opportunity for us to prosper and increase. Whether young or old, every family needs to key into such truths in the Bible for provision, peace, and stability.

Now unto Him (GOD) that is able to do exceeding abundantly above all that we ask or think, according to the power that worketh in us,

Unto Him be glory in the church by Christ Jesus throughout all ages, world without end. Amen.
—Ephesians 3:20—21

Faith in God

There are times when something like an illness in the family could bring a great deal of pressure and tension. During such times, a husband or wife can become irritable and take out his/her frustrations and anxieties on the other spouse. This pressure is particularly so where whatever help they are receiving is not solving the problem. At such times, it is a great comfort to know that there is one final port of call where divine help is available.

I recall a family experience several years ago when one of our children was sick. With both parents as doctors, medical therapy was readily available. But the fever persisted despite all medications. The presentation of the febrile illness was strange. The child would be playing and still be running temperatures of between 39 and 40 degrees Celsius. Different drugs could not bring down the fever, and antibiotics did not help. Around midnight, my wife woke me up to say that the child's body had become quite hot again. As soon as I heard that, I sensed a stirring inside of me, in my inner man. It was as if the Lord was saying to me, "do something about it." I carried the child to the living room, stood there before the Lord, and rebuked the fever in the name of Jesus. The healing was instantaneous. The temperature just went down, and the child's body became normal. The fever never returned. I was grateful to God that He is beyond the very best that we could offer the child as doctors. Because of this power of God at work in us as believers in Christ Jesus, the Apostle Paul said in Philippians 4:13: "I can do all things through Christ who strengthens me."

We may not think a great deal about ourselves usually. However, as born again Christians, we should know that God is at work in us both to will and to do His good pleasure, according to Philippians chapter 2, verse 13.

That God can do all things He desires to do, is always a source of great confidence and stability in marriage for those who belong to Him through faith in Christ Jesus. It tells a Christian couple that they are not alone; neither have they been left alone to grapple with life and love's challenges.

Our Lord Jesus's words in Mark 10:27 brings much faith and comfort with it, as couples go through their lives together. Said our Lord Jesus: *"With men, it is impossible, but not with God; for with God, all things are possible."*

A couple will find their ability to relate in love consistently, very sorely tested by life's circumstances. But God's presence and power at work in them will help them succeed in their marriage no matter their challenges.

God's Expectations

Parents who have raised children naturally have expectations of them. God, as our Father in Heaven, has no less. The Bible puts it this way:

There hath no temptation taken you but such as is common to man: but God is faithful, who will not suffer you to be tempted above that ye are able; but will with the temptation also make a way to escape, that ye may be able to bear it.—1 Corinthians 10:13 (KJV)

This expectation weighs heavily on our hearts, particularly in times of stress and tension. We rise to bring God glory when we realize that He depends on us to reveal the beauty of His life in us, and the power of biblical principles to order our world in different life situations. This grace is shown either by bolstering our sagging spirits through inner peace and strength or cooling our boiling tempers through self-control. The realization that the Holy Spirit is standing by us to help us not fail God spurs us on to respond to our marriage partners the way we should with wisdom, calm, and patience, no matter the situation. Indeed there is great joy when we respond the way we should to our spouses under the prompting of the Holy Spirit of God that is in us, particularly in very trying circumstances.

However, because we are humans, we are bound to fall short of expectation now and again. But with each passing day, we learn how to draw more effectively from God's omnipotence so that our responses would be more consistent and genuinely mirror that of our Father who is in heaven, who is unchanging, and with whom nothing is impossible.

God's Omniscience

We have a lot said on the relevance of tapping from or into the reservoir of knowledge in God's all-knowing mind. This ability is because of the linkage that begins at the new birth. It is vital to note that we must learn to live pre-emptively if we desire to benefit from this reservoir of knowledge maximally. The experience we receive from the Lord should help us prevent instability and other problems within a marriage, rather than wait to solve them after they have occurred.

The Bible reveals that the Lord guides us more to prevent problems than to solve crises. I believe this is why, lead us not into temptation, came before, deliver us from evil, in our Lord's prayer. The more I study events in the Bible, the more convinced I become about this. In the Gospel, according to Matthew, chapter 2, angels of the Lord could have been positioned to defend the baby Jesus from the murderous intentions of Herod, the king. But it was infinitely simpler to guide Joseph, his earthly father, to escape to Egypt with the baby and his mother, Mary.

Those who maintain this spiritual communion with God's Spirit discover that the road to stability and love within marriage is made easier by the day through preventive insights and instructions. We sing a song that says: "The Lord knows the way through the wilderness, (of life). All we have to do is to follow (Him)."

I have found communion with God indispensable to family relationships. Often my prayer to God is: "Lord, I have never been this way before. Please show me exactly what to do." The conclusion I have come to over the years is that the human mind's resources are not sufficient to make life's decisions, for the simple reason that we do not have all the information we need to make decisions. Therefore, the advantage of communion with the Holy Spirit is that we can tap into God's omniscient mind and integrate the past, the present, and the future in the decisions we make daily. Granted that this integration may not be that obvious when we are making the decisions, but hindsight usually would confirm that the Lord indeed led us. For the same reason, I consider conversational prayer a *sine qua non* for successful Christian living.

SINGLES

There is a sense in which a single born again Christian can be said to have a golden opportunity to avoid costly mistakes. I must hasten to add that avoiding those expensive mistakes has its inherent constraints, and we must look at the two sides properly.

UNEQUAL YOKE

The idea of the unequal yoke is in Paul's second letter to the Corinthian Church.

Be ye not unequally yoked together with unbelievers; for what fellowship hath righteousness with unrighteousness? And what communion hath light with darkness?

And what concord hath Christ with Belial? Or what part hath he that believeth with an infidel?

—1 Corinthians 6:14-15 (KJV)

I have heard people say that applying this to marriage is plain discrimination, bigotry, or prejudice based on religion. Indeed, it would appear so until you begin to analyze the basis of it.

When the Bible asks, "What concord hath Christ with Belial? Or what part hath he that believeth with an infidel?" We see that it has to do with the spiritual orientation of the two parties. A person who is born again accepts Jesus Christ as Lord and Saviour. To that individual, the Bible is the final authority for all conduct. The principles revealed in the Bible are to determine our behavior in every area of life. That individual has a biblical orientation to life; the Holy Spirit of God is his or her guide (John 16:13), and the angels of God are ministering spirits to him or her (Hebrews 1:13-14).

A Christian's faith rests on Bible truths. When such an individual marries someone who would prefer to consult the oracle or visit mediums, a conflict is created immediately, which may tear the marriage apart. Such a home would have become converted into a battleground for spiritual forces. Anyone who understands the pattern of response by spiritual forces can only imagine the struggle and conflicts the couple in question would experience in such situations. Sometimes the price such a couple would pay for allowing such a match could be fatal.

The way to look at it is that a person making sacrifices to idols while consulting the oracle is contacting demon spirits. And here is the biblical position on that from 1 Corinthians 10:20-21 (KJV):

B*ut I say that the things which the Gentiles sacrifice,*

they sacrifice to devils, and not to God; and I would not say that ye should have fellowship with devils.

Y*e cannot drink the cup of the Lord and the cup of devils: ye cannot be partakers of the Lord's table and the table of devils. Do we provoke the Lord to jealousy? Are we stronger than he?*
—1 Corinthians 10:20-21

If that same person then goes to God in prayer, seeking the Spirit of God's intervention, what they end up arousing, is God's jealousy, which invariably brings judgment on their lives as revealed in Exodus 20:2-6.

"I am the LORD your God who brought you out of Egypt, where you were slaves. "Worship no god but Me. "Do not make for yourselves images of anything in heaven or on earth or in the water under the earth. Do not bow down to any idol or worship it, because I am the LORD your God and I tolerate no rivals. I bring punishment on those who hate Me and on their descendants down to the third and fourth generation. But I show My love to thousands of generations of those who love Me and obey My laws. (TEV)

To create a situation where two opposing spiritual forces are made to, as it were, compete for our loyalty, is to tear our lives to shreds. It is under such circumstances as these that calamities could overtake families totally without warning, to their utter bewilderment.

UNEQUAL YOKE—NOMINAL CHRISTIANITY AND OTHER MONOTHEISTIC RELIGIONS

It is best to avoid cross-spiritual entanglements. We can also get tangles when we marry someone who is not our travel companion in the journey of life. What is generally described as nominal Christianity can also pose its challenges because of the depth of loyalty and commitment to Christ as Lord and Saviour. "There are good people everywhere," someone may say. Perhaps so, but the journey of life can last forty, fifty, and some 60 years and counting. To travel that long and that far without building soul ties will be a real challenge. Soul ties are tough to make when values and priorities are so divergent.

Issues often come to a head when the Christian in such a relationship opts for active faith in God through Christ. Anyone who has been through this kind of experience will recognize the tremendous stress that it involves. What happens usually is that the two individuals start to pull apart. This loosening of ties is inevitable because loyalty to Christ and His principles must of necessity create a divide between light and darkness. Our Lord Jesus Himself said as much:

"Do not think that I have come to bring peace to the world. No, I did not come to bring peace, but a sword. I came to set sons against their fathers, daughters against their mothers, daughters-in-law against their mothers-in-law; your worst enemies will be the members of your own family. "Those who love their father or mother more than Me are not fit to be My disciples; those who love their son or daughter more than Me are not fit to be My disciples. Those who do not take up their cross and follow in My steps are not fit to be My disciples. Those who try to gain their own life will lose it; but those who lose their life for my sake will gain it.
—Matthew 10:34-39 (TEV)

There are several other practical dimensions to the unequal yoke scenario. For instance, one may find that going to the club for recreation on Sunday mornings, a pastime hitherto enjoyed by all the family, is no longer possible because one of the parties would prefer to go to church to pray and hear the word of God preached. Every aspect of family life is bound to be affected sooner or later. Thoroughly blue and semi-blue television and video shows, which had been fun hitherto, would be seen differently by one of the parties. The unwholesome videos will sting the soul of a believer in Christ, wholeheartedly engaged in holiness. Silly and dirty jokes will now be termed "corrupt communications," in line with Ephesians 4:29. The list of potential stress situations is endless, and the born again believer in a union like this tends to turn into a local home preacher where the situation permits.

But it is at the spiritual level that the issues become clearly defined. Fortunately, matters in the spirit realm are either black or white, good or evil, light or darkness. There are no grey areas out there. Once we understand the way things are there, then we would appreciate the issue of spiritual loyalties.

For these reasons and more, a born again Christian who is single is always advised to avoid unequal yokes. To insist that their unequal yoke would be the exception that proves the rule is merely romantic.

Those who decide to go ahead with their unequal yoke relationship are bound to compromise their Christian principles much sooner than later. But then, someone might say, "and why not? Making compromises is, after all, a sign of maturity. Whether born again or not, everyone is bound to make compromises here and there in marriage."

Undoubtedly, one is bound to agree in a general sense that the ability to make compromises is indeed a sign of maturity. Yes indeed, everyone, whether born again or not, is bound to make adjustments in marriage here or there. But the question is, what sort of changes would these be? There are adjustments, and there are adjustments! Although challenging, some psycho-social adjustments may still be considered mild from a spiritual perspective, mainly when they border on preferences, habits, and the like. But when changes involve spiritual allegiances, powerful forces beyond our control come into play immediately. Therefore, a Christian should appreciate that conflicts in spiritual principles and laws affect human destiny. And these were they potentially exist should make unequal yokes unacceptable.

Following different paths

Sometimes the pressures of love and physical attraction have compelled intending couples to extract a promise that their spiritual lives would follow different directions. This compromise has always proved theoretical to no small extent, as children born into such homes are torn apart by the struggle of husband and wife to secure them for their point of view. This 'tug of love and loyalty' is how stress and tension can emerge in a reasonably stable home environment. Besides, children growing up in such an environment end up being confused, torn apart by each parent's desire to win them over to their point of view. They may end up with no real point of view and might turn their backs on the Lord Jesus because their parents never pointed consistently in any definite direction to experience Him.

Because our spiritual allegiance determines our eternal destiny, nobody should ever contemplate renouncing their faith. It is better to enter into heaven emotionally maimed than to enjoy emotional stability and lose one's soul (Matthew 5:29-30). Anyone who understands the role of forgiveness of sins in Christ Jesus in the relationship between God and man knows that there is no alternative solution to human sinfulness.

Neither is there salvation in any other: for there is none other name under Heaven given among men, whereby we must be saved.
Acts 4:12

Jesus saith unto him I am the way, the truth, and the life: no man cometh unto the Father but by Me.
—John 14:6

This exclusive claim may sound extremist and exclusive. But the reason is not too difficult to appreciate. Religions have always been what men do to please God. Christianity admits that all human effort has failed to meet God's standards of holiness.

As a result, God provided a way of escape in Christ.

This way is why the Bible speaks of those who have gone to take refuge in Christ in Hebrews chapter 6, verse 18.

Revelations chapter 20, verse 15, spells out the issue of man's eternal destiny outside of God's mercy in Christ Jesus. "And whosoever was not found written in the book of life was cast into the lake of fire."

KNOWING THE TIME OF YOUR VISITATION

From the problem of the unequal yoke, we must hurry to the question of timely decisions. Nobody can deny the pressures that can build up over time when decisions to marry are often put off unduly, often without reference to the Spirit of God's inner voice. I had counseled some single ladies in their mid-thirties who recall the time in their lives when suitors beat the path to their doorsteps in an unending stream. Sometimes out of immaturity or ignorance, they had let those opportunities slip by them, only to face frustration later in life.

As I write this, I recall the words of Jesus as he went from Judaea to Jerusalem the week before He was crucified. The scenario reported here in Luke 19:41-44 is quite moving:

And when he was come near, he beheld the city, and wept over it,

Saying, If thou hadst known, even thou, at least in this thy day, the things which belong unto thy peace! but now they are hid from thine eyes.

For the days shall come upon thee, that thine enemies shall cast a trench about thee, and compass thee round, and keep thee in on every side,

And shall lay thee even with the ground, and thy children within thee; and they shall not leave in thee one stone upon another; because thou knewest not the time of thy visitation. (KJV)

One can sense this tragedy of a missed opportunity in the words of Jesus. Young people must always pray for the grace to discern this period of visitation in their lives. The Spirit of the Lord is well able to distinguish what constitutes a divinely orchestrated visitation from what is no more than a carnal lustful "rush."

I recall that this phase of our lives took place while we were in the university or forging a career. This period is usually when young men are beginning to think seriously about sailing away into the future with the girl of their dreams. Many of my friends married their love from college days, and a great many of those relationships are intact today. I meet ladies who regret that they had no time for "So-and-so" because they did not look promising at the time, but who wonder at their error now that "So-and-so" has made good, and seems smashingly different from the gaunt-looking fellow of yesteryears.

I have watched this theory play out in the lives of many young people I know. I have seen ladies that command a queue of suitors. These young men line up one after the other to ask for their hand. I have been privileged to confer with some of these ladies; I have always counseled them to thoughtfully and prayerfully ask the Lord for guidance and help with the decision. At no time in the life of a young lady has Solomon's wisdom on life's decisions been so relevant. Said the wise king in the Book of Proverbs:

Trust in the LORD with all thine heart, and lean not unto

thine own understanding. In all thy ways acknowledge Him, and He shall direct thy paths.

-Proverbs 3:5-6

This problem also occurs in young men, but admittedly, the impact is not as severe, since it is the young man that must seek and find a wife.

For the ladies, however, the pressure can build up over time, and sometimes it can prove a great source of instability in their spiritual life. Some have had to wonder how seriously to take the injunction of unequal yoke when they are in danger of not yoking.

HOW DID I GET HERE AND HOW DO I GET OUT?

A thorough and objective appraisal of one's life is usually the first thing that will help. Following this should be a spirit of meekness that will make us repent of the past errors, which may bother on pride in the way we dismissed prospective suitors earlier. With repentance should follow a dedication to living one's life exclusively for God's glory. This often tends to elicit compassion from the throne of grace, leading to a breakthrough. But more on this later.

Unequal Yoke Dilemma

We cannot leave this issue without putting it squarely in perspective. For some or many, the question often boils down to this: "Should I marry this man or this lady, even though he or she is not particularly as Christian as I would expect him or her to be, and knowing what I know about the imperatives of the new birth, particularly its eternal consequences?"

In this book, by the grace of God, you will find principles based on the Word of God. The benefits and testimonies arising from accepting these principles are also set out in order. But the decision about what you end up doing with your life, knowing all these things must remain yours. By God's grace, what we have shared here will help you make the right decisions for your life and future and, hopefully, at the right time.

However, one thing must be said and said very clearly: "No one who has tasted of God's grace and love in Christ Jesus should go back on that confession of Jesus as Lord of his or her life under any circumstances. No matter the pressure, and no matter the constraints, Jesus should always remain your Lord and Savior."

This is the way the Bible puts it:

It is impossible for those who were once enlightened, tasted of the heavenly gift, and were made partakers of the Holy Ghost,

And have tasted the good word of God, and the powers of the world to come. And if they shall fall away, to renew them again unto repentance; seeing they crucify to themselves the Son of God afresh, and put Him to an open shame.

—Hebrews 6:4-6

Again it says:

Cast not away, therefore, your confidence, which hath great recompense of reward. For ye have need of patience, that, after ye have done the will of God, ye might receive the promise.

—Hebrews 10: 35-36

THE MARRIED—INITIAL CONSIDERATIONS

Given all the problems that affect spiritually mismatched marriages, is there any conceivable reason why anybody should desire to rock their marriage boat by becoming born again? Wouldn't it be more sensible to let sleeping dogs lie and avoid stirring the mud?

Indeed, if the issues were simply that of peace, even if it is the graveyard's proverbial peace, then one may honestly wish matters were better left as they were, particularly for those who have achieved a measure of harmony. There is enough trouble already without trying to add more.

However, there is more than enough stress in many homes that many are desperately searching for a way out.

A beautiful woman was introduced to me one day in a certain place. I had known her husband many years earlier when he was much younger. The gentleman who introduced us, on seeing that I appeared to know the husband fairly well, confided that she had attempted suicide twice before because of her husband's infidelity. I could not believe it. She looked like a queen beside her husband, and one would naturally think that he would adore her because of her good looks and his lack of it. But I was told he was so cruel to her and crushed her feelings by his audacity, often bringing his girlfriends to the marital bed. It was a great pity.

There is no doubt that there are a great many families where there is much suffering today. Knowing and accepting Jesus as Lord and Saviour introduce some order by making the Bible, the eternal word of God, the reference standard for family relationships. Obedience to the Bible's order for families by both the husband and the wife usually will cause their life and circumstances to gravitate to God's control, leading to peace and harmony. The journey is always more comfortable if the husband and wife embrace faith in Christ at the same time. That should reduce the stresses of spiritual incompatibility and personality conflicts significantly. But where they don't, then the onus must be on the one who embraced the faith first, to bear the burden of or pay the price for the desired objective.

Ignorance of this very fact has led to a great deal of backsliding. I have known people who have gone back from following the Lord because their spouses just would not come along, no matter what they did. Others have returned relatively quickly to their former ways of doing things because their spouses' cruel and unkind ways were being unchallenged. One can hear statements like this: "Before I became a Christian, he or she would not have dared a thing like that; He or she would have known what would have been in store for him or her." I have heard women say: "Ever since I became a Christian, he now thinks I am a fool. He now does as he likes, and often has the guts to come and say that since I am a Christian, I should know that I have to overlook all his bad ways."

I believe one should see marriage in its right perspective. It is, among other things, an institution designed by God to assist us in conforming to Christ's image. Those who cross spiritual lines within marriage do face severe persecution. They may do well to heed the time-honored declarations in God's word that says:

Yea, and all that will live godly in Christ Jesus shall suffer persecution.
—2 Timothy 3:12

It is essential to point out that tenacity of purpose and commitment to Christ's cause have their rewards. With much pain and patience, quite a few suffered to get their families into the sunshine of love and stability, deriving from a fruitful relationship with Christ. The power of the LORD God Almighty works wonders in our experience when we stay committed and faithful despite all odds. The Apostle Peter had this in mind when he wrote:

1 In the same way, you wives must submit yourselves to your husbands, so that if any of them do not believe God's word, your conduct will win them over to believe. It will not be necessary for you to say a word,

2 because they will see how pure and reverent your conduct is.
—1 Peter 3:1-2 (TEV)

I once read the story of a lady who attended a ladies' prayer meeting, where she gave her life to Christ. Hitherto her husband would describe her as "thunder and lightning" and had decided to ignore her most of the time. But after this experience, she changed her ways remarkably. Her husband was initially taken aback by the depth of the change and the speed of the transformation. He decided that it was a new form of madness that should wear off in a short time. After two weeks of close observation, he decided that he needed some of whatever it was that changed his wife.

It might look like a contradiction to urge singles on the one hand not to deliberately add spiritual incompatibility into marriage because of its burdens and complications, and on the other hand, encourage the married to go ahead and do exactly that by getting converted. The reason is that life with Christ is the ultimate life, and one should give anything and everything to gain it. Our Lord Jesus Christ put it this way:

44 "The Kingdom of heaven is like this. A man happens to find a treasure hidden in a field. He covers it up again, and is so happy that he goes and sells everything he has, and then goes back and buys that field.

45 "Also, the Kingdom of heaven is like this. A man is looking for fine pearls,

46 and when he finds one that is unusually fine, he goes and sells everything he has, and buys that pearl.
—Matthew 13:44-46 (TEV)

Asking the married to go ahead and seek the Kingdom of God, knowing fully well that it is likely to introduce new stresses and strains within their marriage relationship, can be akin to going through the darkness to meet the dawn. The light of the glorious Gospel of our Lord Jesus Christ, once it has come to shine on a family, brings so much sunshine and joy that it refocuses the family and charts a new path to peace and harmony. This development is not the sunshine and joy that derive from pleasant circumstances only; it does not come from avoiding difficult so-called no-go areas within the marriage. It derives from the fact that even the no-go areas were impacted by the knowledge of Christ and His ways and the power of the Holy Spirit. Those who have experienced this transformation know that nothing can compare to it.

We must leave the rest of this discussion until later, as most of what needs to be said will apply to singles. For now, let us examine the problem of choosing a marriage partner for those who still have the opportunity to do so.

3

INGREDIENTS OF CHOICE OF A MARRIAGE PARTNER

MY IDEAL WIFE/HUSBAND

Some time ago, I discussed with a young man about his "pitiable" state of bachelorhood. I had noted that he had traveled the highway of life for close on 35 years, all alone. I wondered why it was taking him that long to find suitable help. He had his lecture notes on hand and gave me a "one-hour lecture on the sort of woman he was looking for as a life partner. It was a pity because I could not think of anyone I knew with all the qualities stated and the combinations outlined. I knew people who had this and that quality, but no one had all of them put together.

I asked him what he would do if he did not find all those qualities in one person. His answer was quite prompt: "I will keep searching," and I dare say it took a great deal of frustration for him to face the realities of choice of a marriage partner.

It is so easy for fantasy to overtake reason and common sense in choosing a marriage partner. It might be appropriate to say to some men and women: "Please note that some of those people you read about in storybooks and watch in films do not exist in real life."

A young lady was careful to point out to me that, "These young bachelors are not mature. They do not know how to handle a lady." I was also careful to point out that it is most likely that the so-called mature people who know how to handle ladies would be married. They all probably used their wives or former girlfriends to learn how to treat ladies. If you had met them before they had the chance to brush off the rough edges they had acquired in their youth, and possibly in their background, the chances are that you may not have wanted to have anything to do with them. But as they are now, after many seasons have passed over their lives, and after they had shed their midnight tears, they look remarkably like ripe fruits ready to be plucked and prepared to be eaten. If you bothered to ask their wives or the girlfriends who got so frustrated and left, they would tell you that it was not easy. But having passed through the Holy Spirit's pruning school, they now look like they could never have hurt a fly.

This delightful nature also happens with the ladies. There is no doubt that some husbands have many stories locked away in their hearts. The result of all that best-forgotten secret is their beautiful wife of today.

A person may say in retrospect: "I know for sure that the Lord gave me the sort of woman or the sort of man that I needed in my life, and I am grateful." I doubt that they could have said so in many words before they were married for ten years. If they did, it probably would be only a confession of faith. The reason is that at the time they were getting married, they hardly knew their wives or husbands. They had not had the opportunity to see them in different life circumstances for the treasure they carry within them to shine forth. Of course, one is aware that people make such statements rather hastily in the euphoria of the moment and have to wait for years to make it in earnest and with matured and informed understanding.

A young man in search of a wife said to an older man: "You are quite lucky to have your wife. If I could find someone like your wife, I would marry her." The older man replied: "What do you know about my wife; who told you your life could fit into someone like her or vice versa?"

Everyone is entitled to his or her dream. A young lady is allowed to have her dream of a "prince charming" who would sweep her off her feet and cause her to have goose flesh anytime he is around. A young man is allowed to dream about his princess with whom he will sail away into life forever. But in the middle of all these dreams, we must be reminded that these fantasies are about real, fallible, and fault-ridden human beings who are very, very far from being perfect either physically or behaviorally.

Besides, we have no way of looking into the future to determine whether our prospective spouse will stay faithful to us through thick and thin. There is nothing that can tell us that this is the marriage for us, outside of the Lord. So then, how on earth do we know who we are to marry? And without a shadow of a doubt, it is "the million-dollar question" of this subject matter.

CHOICE—WHAT HAS GOD TO DO WITH IT?

If marriage is a relationship between mortals, what has God to do with it? Some wonder why a simple emotional connection should be made spiritual.

A study of the Book of Genesis reveals that marriage was initially God's idea. In Genesis chapter 2, verse 18, the Lord God Almighty said, "it is not good for the man to be alone." As a result of that compassion for Adam's loneliness, the Lord declared: "I will make him a helpmeet (suitable) for him."

To produce this help, the Lord had to put Adam to sleep, suggesting by that action that He did not need Adam's opinion to create a suitable helper for him.

After Adam recovered from 'anesthesia' and saw Eve, he was delighted and expressed his delight with these words:

"This is now bone of my bones and flesh of my flesh..."

One of the recurring thoughts of God's creative process was this: "And God saw that it was good." If finding a suitable help for Adam was right, then, when God did it, it should still be good enough for us today.

The release of the human will from divine control, which occurred at the fall of man in the garden of Eden, is a new factor in man's decision-making process. To achieve the same thing that the Lord did for Adam today, a man now has to cooperate with God willingly. "Divine anesthesia" can only now be administered as it were, to those who are ready for it, those who have decided to let the Lord lead them in the choice of their marriage partner.

WHY DID GOD ARRANGE MARRIAGE?

During the wedding service's admonition phase, companionship and procreation are the two reasons readily adduced for marriage. But there is a third vital reason, highly significant from a strategic perspective. The man was commissioned by God in Genesis chapter 1, verses 26-30, to rule His creation. Under man's authority, the devil's influence on earth was to be neutralized. With God's commission firmly in his hands, the man was to dictate life on planet earth following the divine will. He was to protect God's creation from demonic meddling (Romans 8:19).

After Adam's creation, the Lord observed that he needed someone like him to cope with his rulership's physical, spiritual, and emotional stresses.

The Lord knew that the devil would come against him with many temptations like bestiality and masturbation, and similar sexual perversions, as alternatives for his emotional needs. To meet Adam's personal needs in a way that will be acceptable to God's holiness, God created a woman for him. Adam was to find the emotional and intellectual support he needed to rule the world, in the relationship with his wife, thereby fulfilling God's original intention.

On the side, it is interesting to note that the fall of man did not come from a wrong sexual or emotional relationship. It came from the aspiration to godhood mentioned in Genesis chapter 3, verse 5. "...ye shall be as gods knowing good and evil." This aspiration to godhood was the one area that pitched the man against God's exclusive authority.

Therefore, we may conclude that the wife a young man is looking for is that woman who would complement him in being what God expects them to be, fulfilling their role in God's rulership intent through man.

Those who use their marriage as a springboard for a balanced and deepening spiritual experience may enjoy it physically, intellectually, and emotionally. The couple will discover that the treasures and benefits from such a balanced relationship enable them to grow stronger in the Lord and the power of His might (Ephesians 6:10). The two that become one are stronger in the LORD and are more effective in exercising spiritual authority in the world. Through combined faith and complementary efforts, godliness will increase their effectiveness in the world as servants of God Almighty.

HOW DO I KNOW WHO TO MARRY?

There is a story in the Bible that assists us in no small way to gain some useful insight. It is the story of Isaac's marriage to Rebecca recorded in Genesis 24:1-67. Isaac did not face the challenge of making this decision because of his father, Abraham. Abraham transferred that responsibility to his eldest servant, but with specific guidelines. There are some parents today, I am sure, who would wish that life was still as simple as in the days of Isaac when young men and women left such issues to their parents to decide.

However, in how the servant made his choice, we learn the lesson and gain the insight we need. The guidelines were quite clear.

- Do not take a wife unto my son of the daughters of the Canaanites among whom I dwell (Verse 3).

- Go unto my country, and to my kindred, and take a wife unto my son Isaac.

Abraham's "bigoted" view of things may not be that obvious from this passage, but in the laws given to his descendants by God through Moses, we begin to gain some useful understanding. The Lord forbade the children of Israel from marrying the sons and daughters of Canaan. The reason was stated in Deuteronomy, chapter 7.

Neither shalt thou make marriages with them; thy daughter thou shalt not give unto his son, nor his daughter shalt thou take unto thy son.

For they will turn away thy son from following Me, that they may serve other gods; so will the anger of the Lord be kindled against you, and destroy thee suddenly.

—Deuteronomy 7:3-4 (KJV)

Looking at Abraham's other instructions, we conclude that this so-called bigoted view of marriage is not informed by tribe nor language, nor by ethnicity, culture, or race. It stems from this overbearing desire in Abraham to preserve the correct knowledge and worship of the LORD God Almighty in his descendants.

Abraham judged that if Isaac took a wife from Canaan where he lived, the local idols' overwhelming influence, coming through his wife with whom he would share deep intimacy, might prove too strong for him to resist. Therefore, he foresaw the demise of God's true worship in his lineage within one generation. This threat or danger was why he insisted that Isaac must not marry from the locals. But the same thing would also happen were Isaac to return to Abraham's birthplace in Syria, to live with his wife. His wife would be living among her people and might find the local idol worship irresistible. Either way, the true worship of God would have been in danger.

A Christian may marry anyone from any part of the world, provided the marriage so contracted will not prove a threat to God's true worship in his or her life and that of coming generations. God blessed Abraham and his unborn generations because he loved the Lord with all his heart, and as the Lord predicted about him in Genesis. 18:19, he instructed his descendants to preserve the true worship of God after he was gone.

For I know him, that he will command his children and his household after him, and they shall keep the way of the Lord, to do justice and judgment; that the Lord may bring upon Abraham that which he hath spoken of him
—Genesis 18:19 (KJV)

We need to bear in mind that the blessings of the Lord are always conditional. The reason is that they are invariably part of a covenant. To receive the benefit, they must note the covenant's conditions and be careful to fulfill them. Abraham was blessed of the Lord all right. But verse 19 of Genesis chapter 18 tells us why. The blessing was conditional when the Bible said, "That the Lord may bring upon Abraham that which He hath spoken to him," after he has carefully instructed his descendants to follow the Lord to do justice and judgment according to the commandments of the Lord. Those who neglect this fact pave the way to a great deal of frustration in their lives.

Having decided to marry someone from anywhere provided the relationship so contracted would lead to the preservation of God's true worship in your life and lineage; How do you go on to find the person? But just before we do that, we may need to stop for a little while and examine a few issues that bear directly on the question of choosing a marriage partner.

THE RACIAL AND ETHNIC QUESTION

It is interesting to note that racial and ethnic divides exist all over the world to various degrees. The Apostle Paul rebuked the Corinthian church for their divisions, which he felt revealed their spiritual immaturity (1 Corinthians 3:1-3)

Those who have problems with race and the ethnic question must remember that racial superiority is historically determined. The barbarians of one age, may have been the dominant civilization of yesteryears. In the Bible New testament days, the Europeans were the barbarians, and the kings and queens of the day were Semitic or African. Today, the story is different, but who knows tomorrow?

The Gospel continues to shine a constant and consistent light on human behavior, pointing the way forward towards the fullness of Christ. The apostle Peter declared in Acts 10:34 & 35: "*...Of a truth, I perceive that God is no respecter of persons: But in every nation, he that feareth Him, and worketh righteousness, is accepted with Him.*"

It should be clear to any group that fails to recognize the divine intent in the above statement, that much sooner than later, they will lose relevance in heaven in the divine scheme of things, and then, they will lose relevance on earth. What the world needs are men who know God. And anyone who knows God will submit to the authority of God's word in its entirety. Paul's remark to the Galatians should help any individual climb out of a racial or ethnic pit.

For ye are all the children of God by faith in Christ Jesus. For as many of you as have been baptized into Christ have put on Christ. There is neither Jew nor Greek; there is neither bond nor free, there is neither male nor female: for ye are all one in Christ Jesus. And if ye be Christ's, then are ye Abraham's seed, and heirs according to the promise.
-Galatians 3:26-29 (KJV)

A Christian's neighborhood from where to pick a wife or husband should have neither racial nor ethnic boundaries. But that is not to say that it is everybody who can successfully build a cross-cultural relationship. It poses several challenges of its own, and only those led by the Lord should go into it.

UNEQUAL YOKE AMONG CHRISTIANS?

When the Bible says, do not be unequally yoked together with unbelievers in 2 Corinthians, chapter 6, verse 14, we understand that when applied to marriage, it would be referring to a union between a Christian and an unbeliever. It would, therefore, seem a contradiction in terms to speak of unequal yoke among Christians.

The question asked in this context is this: "Does this mean that any Christian can be your wife or husband provided he or she confesses to having faith in our Lord Jesus Christ as Lord and Savior?" One may answer "yes," to this question, but only hypothetically because we know that people are still different despite being Christians. In other words, Christianity, as a faith, does not produce a single "ultra-blendable" type of personality. As has often been said in our local parlance, "as the prints on our fingers are different, so are we."

Therefore, we must accept our individuality by agreeing that even among Christians, it is not just anyone and everyone who can share the deep intimacy of marriage with you. These differences have led to the emergence of the COMPATIBILITY FACTOR, which is a way of admitting the personality differences between individuals, even among Christian individuals.

I suppose the compatibility factor loosens us from the constricting grips of the notion that "it is only one person and one person alone that I can marry in this world." It is essential to know this because we do experience rejection in the pursuit of a marriage partner. Because we are talking about matching personalities and factors of individuality, it stands to reason that several individuals can make reasonably good compatible matches with a single individual. It also stands to reason that there must be one person who will prove the best match, all things put together, and the desire and prayers of every person is to match with their best option or their best possible mate. To be matched with your best potential mate, all things considered, requires us to be very sensitive and obedient to the Holy Spirit.

But the question remains: "How do I find this person, and where is he or she hiding?"

GUIDANCE TO THE BEST CHOICE

Shakespeare said that there is no art to know the mind's construction in the face, or words to that effect. I suppose he could easily have been echoing the prophet Jeremiah in the Bible, where he said: "The heart is deceitful above all things, desperately wicked: who can know it?" (Jeremiah 17:9).

Some time ago, I came across the story of a Christian young lady's experience. A young man, supposedly Christian and born again, was courting her, and marriage preparations were in progress. Suddenly events began to warn her that this young man might not be as Christian as he claimed. She decided to pay him a few surprise visits, and her fears proved right. Most Sunday mornings, she found him at home in bed, with one excuse or the other. She wondered, "whether this potential head of the home can lead us all to God."

Unknown to her, some of her friends had noticed this man's ways and started to pray that the good Lord would help her see what they had seen. When she noticed these traits, she began to pray that the Lord would reveal things the way they are. Not too long after, events overtook this young man, and he confessed that he was only pretending to be Christian or born again and that there was no way he could have kept up with that kind of lifestyle for long. The young lady broke the engagement when the danger signals became obvious. The Lord honored her commitment, and not long after that, she was on her way to the altar with another eligible young man.

Abraham's servant in Genesis 24, was faced with this kind of dilemma. How on earth do I know who to bring back for my master's son Isaac?

And he said, O Lord God of my master Abraham, I pray thee, send me good speed this day and show kindness to my master Abraham.

Behold, I stand here by the well of water, and the daughters of the men of the city come out to draw water;

And let it come to pass, that the damsel to whom I shall say. Let down thy pitcher, I pray thee, that I may drink; and she shall say. Drink, and I will give thy camels drink also; let the same be she THAT THOU

HAST APPOINTED FOR THY SERVANT ISAAC; and thereby shall I know that thou hast showed kindness unto my master.
—Genesis 24:12-14 (KJV)

We may do well to note how this gentleman resolved this dilemma. He prayed a simple prayer, "Lord, I need to know the young lady that you have appointed for Isaac." The voice of young men should rise to heaven in prayer for themselves; "Lord, I need to know the young woman that you have appointed for me."

Having said this prayer, the gentleman devised some recognition signal. "Lord," he prayed, "this young lady should offer me water to drink, and beyond that, she should also offer to water my animals too."

We often have problems with the recognition signals we put before the Lord to determine His mind on this kind of question because they are too general to assist us in making the decision. Abraham's servant could easily have said: "Lord, let the lady be the one that will answer Shalom! when I say, Shalom!" Assuming that was the standard greeting, an individual would be right to wonder if this usual greeting would be enough to make such a decision.

Besides, some people play an old trick. The first lady that comes call her Miss A, may say "Shalom." They may then decide to take one good look at her, and if they do not like what they see, they may conclude that her "Shalom" was somewhat hesitant. They may then go on to define the way to say the Shalom. It must be full-throated and boisterous and must draw out a courteous bow. What often happens is that Miss B then turns up with a full-throated Shalom and a bow. Again they look up, and if they do not like what they see, they say that Shalom is such an easy recognition signal that one shouldn't judge with it. But soon after they have decided to throw away their recognition signal, a certain Miss C emerges with a full-throated Shalom and a courteous bow, just like Miss B. Because they like what they see of Miss C, they jump at her, deciding that Shalom is, after all, a good signal. Sometimes, they go on to defend the indefensible by saying that Miss C's Shalom was much deeper and more boisterous than that of the previous two and that her bow was from her heart—indeed, it was. You may hear something like: "Oh the way she did it, and how she said it was different. It was more graceful. One could see the sincerity very readily in all her gestures."

Based on this kind of conviction, they may proceed to court Miss C and marry her. It is often subsequent events in their marriage experience that will compel them to admit that they had indulged in self-deception concerning that exercise.

Undoubtedly, after Abraham's servant had offered his prayers with the recognition signal that would be quite unusual, he waited with trepidation to know how the Lord was going to answer the prayer. He did not have to wait for long.

And it came to pass before he had done speaking, that,

behold, Rebekah came out, who was born to Bethuel, son of Milcah, the wife of Nahor, Abraham's brother, with her pitcher on her shoulder.

And the damsel was very fair to look upon, a virgin, neither had any man known her; and she went down to the well, and filled her pitcher, and came up.

And the servant ran to meet her and said. Let me, I pray thee, drink a little water of thy pitcher.

And she said, Drink, my Lord: and she hasted, and let down her pitcher upon her hand, and gave him drink.

And when she had done giving him drink, she said, I will draw water for thy camels also, until they have done drinking.

And she hasted, and emptied her pitcher into the trough, and ran again unto the well to draw water, and drew for all his camels.

And the man wondering at her held his peace, to wit whether the Lord has made his journey prosperous or not.
—Genesis 24:15-21 (KJV)

What he made is what you could describe as a "risky" open-ended prayer. Anybody could have walked in through that door. All they needed to do was reply to his request for water in a specific way.

But even after Rebekah answered correctly, Abraham's servant was still wondering whether she was the one. The reason was that she still had to come from the right family. That would be the confirmation he would need to prove that God's hand was indeed in the choice.

The open-ended prayer could have admitted anybody. However, for that anybody to become Mr. Right or Miss Right, they have to pass through a confirmatory test. For Abraham's servant, Rebecca must come from the right family to confirm that she is the one God has appointed for Isaac.

This reserve confirmatory "trump card," as it were, was most significant because the servant did not know any member of Abraham's family; neither did he know the way to their house. He was delightfully surprised by what he discovered. He knew for sure that the Lord had gone ahead of him to make a choice.

Whose daughter art thou? ...
—Genesis 24:23

His heart must have been pounding within him as he waited for her answer. "My God," he must have prayed silently, "Let this be the end of my journey and the beginning of another life for Isaac, Amen."

And she said unto him, I am the daughter of Bethuel, the son of Milcah, which she bare unto Nahor.

And the man bowed down his head and worshipped the Lord.

And he said. Blessed be the Lord God of my master Abraham, who hath not left destitute my master of His mercy and His truth; I BEING IN THE WAY, THE LORD LED ME to the house of my master's brethren.

—Genesis 24:24, 26-27

OTHER WAYS OF KNOWING GOD'S CHOICE

What we have outlined above is one way of discovering the mind of God in matters like this. It is by no means the only way. One common mistake is to insist on one path, ignoring other signals from the Lord.

A careful study of the Bible will reveal that the guidance of the Lord came to His servants in various ways.

DREAMS AND VISIONS

Dreams and visions are other ways through which we can receive the guidance of the Lord. For example, Joseph, the husband of Mary, the mother of Jesus, was led to marry his wife through a dream.

But while he thought on these things, behold, the angel of the Lord appeared unto him in a dream, saying, Joseph, thou son of David, fear not to take unto thee Mary thy wife: for that which is conceived in her is of the Holy Ghost —Matthew 1:20 (KJV)

It would appear from the records that Joseph was guided mainly through dreams (See Matthew 2:13, 19-20, and 22). In an individual's life, some communication channels may be preferred to others by the LORD. Not because of constraints on the part of the LORD but because of limitations within the individual.

However, we may note that the dreams used to guide Joseph were quite specific and to the point. Acting on a non-specific dream or vision will be quite risky, since we do not see such examples in the Bible, and common sense should dictate to the contrary.

However, in the experience of Peter in Acts 10:1-20, we notice that the vision was somewhat non-specific. A sheet came down from heaven containing meat objectionable to a Jew. Peter was commanded in the vision to arise and kill these animals for meat. He objected. He was pointedly told: "What God hath cleansed, that call not thou common." (Verse 15).

He was soon to learn the meaning of this strange vision.

While Peter thought on the vision, the Spirit said unto him. Behold, three men seek thee. Arise therefore, and get thee down, and go with them, doubting nothing: FOR I HAVE SENT THEM."

—Acts 10:19-20 (KJV)

I can believe that Peter could still have been baffled even at this stage until he met the men and heard their story. It was then that the vision made sense. The men were Gentiles, and God had sent them to Peter to ask him to come and preach to them. Ordinarily, Peter would have had difficulties going to the home of a Gentile, but not after a vision like that with the pointed warning: "What God had cleansed, that call not thou common."

THE INWARD WITNESS AND OTHER WAYS

God may also speak to our hearts. I believe that this inward witness should confirm any other mode of communication. Let us note that this inward communion is the by-product of this linkage between the Spirit of God and the spirit in man. We experience this linkage at the new birth, as discussed earlier.

One thing about the inward witness is that it is sensed variously in different individuals. Naturally, the preferred mode of it is the inner dialogue, where discernible and intelligible dialogue exists between the Spirit of God and the spirit in man. It is during this dialogue that we express our reservations and receive His answers. Puzzles and riddles, and steps to the actualization of the union get real-time attention.

Some express this inward witness as a feeling of peace. And by that, they mean that any time a decision is not in line with God's will in their lives, there is a sustained feeling of disquiet within. But a sense of peace tends to confirm to them that they have divine approval.

Some others say that an inward witness is never confirmed for them until the Spirit of God has led them to a passage of the Bible for correlation.

Yet others say that an independent confirmation by a third party must follow this inward peace before they can go ahead with the decision.

Without this third party input as proof of authenticity, they would still doubt the direction suggested by the inward peace.

It is difficult to emphasize one recognition method over another when sensing the divine will in the individual's life. There is a subjective element to this. And that has made many believers distrustful of anyone who claims to be led by the Lord. This distrust may also be because they are yet to start sensing the Spirit's voice in their heart as believers. It may again come from the experience of false claims.

The just shall live by faith, that's the holy writ in Romans 1:17. Learning to hear God, trust God, and obey Him is the core of our Christian experience and journey. Walking by faith in this area of our lives must be encouraged in every believer. I had cause to ask a young lady, with regards to a relationship she was in: "Have you heard anything from the Lord?" She was honest enough to answer, "No." She told me that the gentleman was very kind and loving, and they seemed to get along very well together.

Not too long ago, I confronted a nice-looking young lady about her single status. "What is the problem?" I asked. "Don't the young men have eyes?" I joked. She told me that a young man had been pressuring her to answer his proposal. "And why have you not answered?" I queried. "Are they on a long vacation in heaven?" I joked. She told me that she sensed that the answer was "no." "On what basis?" I inquired further. She then proceeded to tell me of two of her dreams that were quite similar.

I recall the first one vividly. A colleague at work met her with the young man and said to her: "Is this the man? No! You shouldn't marry him. Not this man." She was quite shocked about it because nobody in her office was aware that she was in any relationship. She felt she had the confirmation when another friend, a Christian sister, told her the same thing in a dream. The exciting thing about this story was that the young man in question later came to see me. He told me that the lady had those dreams because, at that time, he had not been born again. When I thought about that, I realized that God's omniscience would have known about his "newfound faith," from the first day of his birth. So I doubted that a double "No," could so easily be explained away.

We must understand and appreciate the depth of God's love for His children. That love guarantees that anyone who sincerely desires to follow the will of the Lord, particularly in this area of their life, will undoubtedly be led. One way or another, the Holy Spirit of God will figure out how to communicate the decision of the Almighty to their heart and mind. The aim is for them to know what the Lord would have them do; what they should do about a pending proposal.

Honesty has never been such a virtue on any question as much as in this area. Our feelings can run ahead of us and create confusion within us. But honesty, what the psalmist referred to as truth in the inward man, (Psalm 51:6) will always deliver us from such a snare.

One conviction that should assure our hearts is that the God who spoke through an ass to the erring prophet Balaam, in Numbers, Chapter 22, verse 28, can help us know His will. If He would cause a floating finger to write on a wall and seal the fate of the morally bankrupt heathen king of Babylon, Belshazzar, in Daniel chapter 5, He sure can use anything and anyone, at anytime, to ensure that we do His will for our lives. To that, we should say a resounding, "Amen."

In the end, the important thing is that we come away with a conviction that this is the direction in which the Lord is leading us in our bid to make a marriage decision.

PERSONAL FEELINGS AND CHOICE

Some feel that there is something unreal about a marriage contracted based on spiritual conviction alone—the inward witness. Man is, after all, made up of body, soul, and spirit. Shouldn't his soul, where his feelings reside, have a say?

I have had young people say to me: "It is impossible to accept someone you have no feelings for, just based on conviction or the inward witness. I do not feel drawn to him or her in any way." There is no doubt that feelings must have a significant part in marriage between two people.

To marry and be happy, they must come to like each other and love each other deeply. There is no doubt, however, that feelings can be quite deceptive. You can feel one way today and another way tomorrow. So if feelings were all there was to it, then one day you would feel like getting married to him or her, the next day, you would not be sure anymore.

Therefore, one would prefer a situation where a more solid spiritual conviction supports the somewhat fragile feeling. For example, one's feelings may change in the middle of an outing because of an incident, which may be trivial. On the spur of the moment, they may decide that the marriage is off to the utter dismay of the other party. The bewildering shock will be the trivial nature of the incident that precipitated the demise of the relationship.

Sometimes, the issues could be much deeper than that. There is this story of a certain gentleman who fell in love with a lady. The lady I understand was quite amiable and friendly and could fit into his highly visible social life. Every road appeared to be leading to the altar until he had an unsolicited nightmare that revealed horrendous spiritual struggles that would occur within the marriage were it to take place. The gentleman sought counsel, and he and his counselor prayerfully concluded that the Lord was not saying "No," to the relationship, but was merely revealing what it would entail. The gentleman opted to look elsewhere. He doubted that he had the faith to go through what he considered a titanic struggle in the spirit realm.

Given this type of experience, feelings alone should not decide on the choice. It certainly should be a significant part of a marriage decision. Sometimes, they are late in coming, and so love has to grow where it was not spontaneous.

I have always felt that whenever feelings are yet to develop, communicating your conviction to the other party should be delayed, no matter how overwhelming the belief in your heart. One should never share a "dry" or unromantic proposal with another person. A lady would rather hear that you love her very much and would like to marry her than that God has sent you to marry her.

I recall what the late Pastor S. G. Elton said to us some years ago. The comment was more for the benefit of the ladies. Said he: "If any of these young men come to you to say, 'the Lord says we should get married.' Tell them: 'Yes, I have heard what the Lord has said, but what do you say yourself?'"

OTHER CONSIDERATIONS

Some people feel that having shared interests should be a crucial factor in a marriage decision. Indeed it should be a factor, but how vital it should be is another matter. Some people believe that sharing a common interest is a significant factor of stability in the home.

We had a good laugh recently at a marriage seminar I was conducting when we looked at various other long-term and short-term factors. We chose hypothetical characters, who were primarily men. The first young man went to the Lord and asked to be led to a beauty queen as a fiancée. The Lord consented and found him a smashing beauty. Soon after they got married, he realized that other people noticed his wife's beauty too. He began to be worried when men came over to greet him each time they went visiting and took the occasion to chat up his wife. The feeling of jealousy gradually took hold of him. Another gentleman wanted a girl that was cerebral and chatty. After they got married, it all worked out well for a while until they quarreled. He could not stand that the lady could match him, wit for wit, word for word. As he thought about the quality he admired so much in her, he felt she should have the good sense to know when not to use it.

The third young man went to the Lord, asking for a prayer warrior, a deeply spiritual woman. The Lord again obliged. But he was shocked the first honeymoon night when the lady stated rather matter of factly, that the very first act of intimacy must be preceded by at least one full day of fasting and prayer to dedicate it.

Common interests certainly would help a relationship that has obtained a nod from heaven. I am one of those who passionately believe that the Lord knows what premium to place on "common interests" in any given relationship. For some people, it may be quite significant. For others, it may not be. Some common interests come alive during courtship; others surface after the wedding.

I recall that my wife and I enjoyed the game of scrabble soon after we got married. I doubt that we have played more than a few games in the last thirty-five years. Raising children and running a private medical practice has eaten away much of the leisure time we used to have.

Abraham's servant discovered that God has a way of taking care of everything necessary to empower us to fulfill destiny when He guides us to make our marriage decisions.

SIGNIFICANT AGE DIFFERENTIAL

The idea of a broad age differential might be entirely subjective. An individual must be prepared to address this issue squarely when faced with the option. To enter into a relationship involving what the individual considers a significant age differential requires some psychological adjustment.

This adjustment is what will help when relatives, friends, and neighbors try to show their disapproval. If the person in such a relationship or union is flustered and embarrassed, rather than enthusiastic, it would mean that they are yet to come to terms with their reality. And that may cause the undoing of the bond.

A friend may bump in on you as an older lady married to a much younger man, and say something like this: "Hello! darling, good to see you looking so well." You then pause to introduce your husband: "Oh, meet..."

"Oh, that must be your brother; I haven't met this one before."

Then you start to say something like: "Oh yes, my brother, of course; But he is also eh..."

"Your son then, or is it your cousin?"

"No! He is my husband."

"Did you say, husband?"

"Yes."

"Oh, dear," the friend goes. "Hello! My name is Fiona. Good to see you."

They may then turn and walk away with that look that says:

"Gosh! This is not right."

A couple in a marriage relationship where the woman is significantly older than the man must adjust their mind to prepare for this scenario. They should know that there will be unkind remarks here and there. Both the man and the woman must be psychologically prepared to cope. His friends may be sneering behind him: "What is in it for him? Has she got a lot of money? Does she have a rich endowment from an indulgent father? Even if she does, is that why he should marry a woman old enough to be his mother?"

Besides the pressures from without, the couple should also be able to cope with the demands arising from having grown up in two different age-grades, with varying perspectives on life and issues. They must be prepared to make allowances for each other.

What I have implied here is that it is not everybody that will have the capacity to enter into a relationship like this. Therefore, the individual must be very sure of his or her convictions. The belief or faith gets tested during courtship with the occasions that call for adaptation. If they are quite confident of what the Lord is saying to them, they must use the courtship period to develop the relationship. No one should rush into this type of relationship. A relationship like this can turn out very stable, happy, and fulfilling all round. Those who enter into it with conviction and love will find peace and joy, too, like any other couple.

The converse situation where a very young lady is marrying a much older man also poses a problem, but not often as big. The pressure will undoubtedly be more on the young lady marrying the older man. The older man involved with her maybe receiving congratulatory notes for his good fortune. A lady said to me some time ago: "These older bachelors need no help from you to go after the young girls. That is what they want."

The pressure is undoubtedly on the girl. Her friends may wonder as well what is in it for her. "Maybe, if the man were a millionaire or something like that," they would sneer. "But to marry a man like that just for money? No."

"Oh, but I love him. He is charming, too," the lady may reply.

"Indeed, he is. I think I can see that too. His bank manager has confirmed the source of his charm."

There is no doubt that a girl in this situation may find more encouragement than a young man in a similar situation. She may find some who would advise her that the men are much more mature this way. Some time ago, I encountered a young lady who decided against a relationship like this because of the children involved. She did not think she had the depth to cope with adolescents from a previous marriage.

The good thing about the Lord is that He knows us more than we can ever know ourselves. I often take encouragement in the Scripture that says:

There hath no temptation taken you but such as is common to man: but GOD IS FAITHFUL, WHO WILL NOT SUFFER YOU TO BE TEMPTED ABOVE THAT YE ARE ABLE; but will with the temptation also make a way to escape, that you may be able to bear it —1 Corinthians 10:13 (KJV)

The reference to this Scripture does not imply that marriage is a temptation, far from it. The inference here is that God will not allow you to go into something you cannot handle. In other words, if God is asking you to enter into this kind of relationship, and is developing love in both your hearts for each other, then you must be among the few who can make a success of it. I know that not every one of us can make all the necessary adjustments required in each of these situations. But those who feel led into it and are willing to make the needed changes will find fulfillment and happiness.

EDUCATIONAL AND SOCIAL DIFFERENCES

This kind of consideration is identical to the one above, but its impact and consequences can be much more severe. A lot of adjustments would be required to make a relationship like this successful. If a lady marries a man of a lower educational and social status, she would have to ensure that this does not color her views of him. If everything he does is followed by: "Well, what does one expect; this is all he can do," then she is creating a problem for herself in the area of obedience and submission. If she always dismisses his views, because he hardly has any insight, condescension will spell disaster. Working at a relationship like this to create happiness and joy will require a great deal of humility on both sides.

A man involved in a relationship of this nature should be humble enough to admit its reality and work hard to bridge the gap that exists as much as possible. There is nothing wrong with bridging such an educational gap through some form of adult education, particularly for someone whose academic progress in life was halted by a lack of opportunity or sponsorship. In this, he should receive a lot of encouragement from his wife. Learning other ways of doing things, if always seen as "trying to get me to do things your way because of my little education" will create monumental problems. To pretend that no gaps exist, or that the differences do not matter, will likely prove disastrous because the individual would not be gearing up to make the necessary adjustments.

I once heard of a man who was reluctant to pursue an adult education program that he was academically well capable of undertaking because he felt his wife was not proud of him. He thought that his wife was trying to produce the sort of husband that she had always wanted. This attitude constitutes a negative complex, and anyone likely to suffer from this kind of insecurity and lack of self-confidence should not go into this kind of relationship.

A couple can bridge a gap like this where there are conviction and love. It is possible to evolve an enviable union that would have gotten rid of the differences' rough edges. Propelled by passion and a determination to achieve harmony in his home, a man in this position should be prepared to make the necessary sacrifices to lead his family from an informed position of strength. That way, the level of communication in the home would be satisfactory to both parties. This effort will reduce or eliminate the temptation to seek a more satisfying company outside the house. This situation, if unresolved, can expose the couple to the possibility of infidelity and sin.

A man marrying below his social and educational status must bear in mind that he has not gone to acquire a domestic hand and a bed mate, designed to be neither heard nor seen in public. Any attempt to do that will create complexes of inadequacy in the person so treated. Such a lady should be encouraged to improve herself as much as possible to reduce stresses within the relationship.

The most common problem area will be communication. To prefer the company of other men and women, as a result, will create tension and possible suspicions of infidelity. This situation can also develop within an old marriage, as one party overtakes the other either educationally or socially. Whether it is within an existing marriage or within one about to emerge, the problems remain identical. Where there are firm conviction and love on both sides, nothing will be impossible, given the abundance of grace that comes through faith in God.

It is important to note that it is not the absolute level of education that is crucial. I have come across people who have bridged their level of informed and expressed opinion considerably without formalizing their knowledge. This achievement is sometimes to a standard or degree that will astound those with more formal education. However, where complexes of inadequacy plague such people, it would be in their interest to formalize their awareness level through certification processes, encouraged by their wives with sensitivity. Women whose husbands are bridging this kind of gap would often say to anyone who cares to listen: "Bob is working on his thesis. He should defend it next semester." This information is always volunteered and sometimes out of context.

LOOKS AND PERSONALITY

These are features that can be said to be in transit as it were. I should know, given the changes I have undergone physically, in the last twenty-some years. I look at some of the photographs I took some years ago, and I can hardly recognize myself—the luxurious black hair with the hairline intact and not a tinge of grey—all that has gone now, giving way to a balding scalp, and a thin fluffy grey. Maybe I am blessed not to have also gone paunchy. If looks and personality had been crucial during my search, maybe people like me with the way I look now may still be waiting in the queue. I know a very tall gentleman with a few wrinkles and a dashing touch of grey. He is always praying. He probably should dye his hair, and maybe reduce his height a little bit. It might help. A young lady said to me the other day concerning looks: "If he does not have the looks but has the brains, then I will ask the Lord to give the children my looks and his brains. That should work out fine." On a more serious note, one must say that these transient considerations should not be at the top of the list of essential factors. Everyone knows that only a few people are ugly and that children are getting prettier with every passing generation. However, we should be honest enough to admit that they are essential because they are the features that generally promote physical attraction. One needs to be emotionally and physically drawn to another to contemplate marriage.

MATERIAL COMFORT

With the global economic changes, particularly here in Nigeria, material comfort has almost taken the eligibility question's front seat. A very viable middle class has all but virtually disappeared due to the recent economic downturn. This situation was not the case a few years back. A young man fresh from national service, or in the graduating class of a higher institution, would be looking forward to joining a reasonably stable middle class. He can bank on getting decent housing, a car, usually procured with his or her employer's assistance, and the typical household appliances like refrigerators, freezers, television, and a stereo set. It was a given that a young man would have all these within a year or two of graduation. Air conditioners came a little later, and most married couples who joined the middle class on leaving school would have installed at least one unit in their bedroom within three to five years of marriage.

A great deal of that has changed now. A young man graduating from a higher institution is no longer confident about finding a job. Graduate unemployment has become a reality. That these things were not like this back in the day proves that it is a changing phase of life and living.

However, faith teaches us that the national economic state does not necessarily dictate a person's financial status. As the preacher is wont to say: "Your case should be different if you believe." One of our Lord Jesus Christ's oft-repeated sayings to people who approached Him in their need was: "Be it unto you according to your faith." (Matthew 9:29). Faith changes things and will continue to change things. The prophet Zechariah declared in chapter 4, verse 10: "Who has despised the day of small things." In another version, it is rendered like this: "Who has despised the days of small beginnings." Sometimes, important things have a way of starting in a corner, and a person must approach a marriage relationship with faith. There is faith, where there is a conviction, and where there is love, then nothing should be impossible for a couple like that. They will attempt the mountain of the Lord's expectations of them on this side of eternity, with some reasonable degree of success.

IS THERE A CHRISTIAN NEIGHBOURHOOD?

I believe one can say yes, with a reasonable degree of conviction, judging from a statistical perspective. If one takes a survey of Christian married couples or even just married couples, it will become evident that there is undoubtedly a neighborhood concept. People marry people they meet in their social environment, work environment, or church and fellowship environment. There always will be exceptions, but undoubtedly the facts are there for all to see.

The individual searching for a marriage partner will find his/her "Christian neighborhood" so-called in the church and the fellowship of believers he or she attends. Others include camps and conferences and even house fellowships, and wherever believers meet generally.

The chances that one's wife or husband will come from outside of their local "Christian neighborhood" is the exception rather than the rule.

When I look back, I immediately realize from my experience and that of my friends in the university, that this factor was valid then as it is now. Over 80 percent of us either married people in the fellowship immediately or soon after.

I recall discussing this point with a single lady not long ago. I had wondered that she did not get engaged to someone while she was in the University Christian Fellowship. She told me that she never thought seriously about marriage those days and that besides, there were no eligible bachelors in the fellowship even if she had thought of it. It is not too difficult to see why this could be so. In the sixties and seventies and the early eighties, a final year graduate student in the university or polytechnic was an eligible bachelor. However, the economic situation in the country has dramatically reduced that eligibility. Besides, the graduating age is getting lower and lower, and people now graduate at under twenty years of age or just a little over twenty. Notwithstanding, commitments could still be made at this age if the people are mature spiritually. The university environment aggregates people of similar academic and intellectual background who generally would have a lot in common.

Some years ago, I had an opportunity to address this issue while talking to a graduating set of Christian students in one of Nigeria's universities. I was reminded of that meeting a few days ago when a young man asked me to preach at his wedding. He told me that his courtship and that of several others like him started after that talk. The girls suddenly realized that they ought to take the local proposals quite seriously since the future is locked up in the hands of the ALMIGHTY GOD. An ineligible bachelor of today could quickly become the most successful entrepreneur of tomorrow.

I had caused another occasion to counsel a young lady to let her behaviour in her local environment speak eloquently of her availability so that the young men who are getting "convictions" about her would be encouraged to approach her. I told her that if she continued to remain aloof, condescending, and patronizing, she might discover that she passed by God's perfect will for her life without even realizing it.

This mistake is familiar to older bachelors and spinsters, some of whom can count opportunities of getting married that they let slip by them.

I quite appreciate the problems a young lady can face with such a degree of openness. One lady told me that it courts disaster since one could easily be harassed beyond measure by so-called prospective suitors, both eligible and ineligible.

Be that as it may, one must continue to be open to the Lord concerning people in their "Christian neighborhood" and reflect such openness to people in their environment as much as possible. That makes it easier for the Lord to meet their need in this area at the first opportunity. There is no doubt that many young men and women will avoid much heartache if this approach to the local environment is adopted. It may not produce the match, but it may speak eloquently of our availability, helping in no small way to make the eventual match.

On a recent visit to a university city here in Nigeria, two young people met me with a lot of gleaming hope in their eyes. One was in an undergraduate class, and the other was at the postgraduate level. They had committed themselves to each other for a future together as husband and wife. It was all by faith, as there was nothing on the ground to say what that future would look like, save many potentials buried in well-respected educational qualifications. But there is no doubt that they had crossed a significant milestone of their lives by that decision, and now have the opportunity of building up a team for God quite early in their lives. They could have left the issue until they arrived at a broader, more diverse, and diffuse social environment, where more difficulties abound. Utilizing the opportunity of their "current Christian neighborhood" provided the opportunity for the Lord to meet the need in this area of their lives.

However, one must emphasize that this may not necessarily be so for every person, but neglecting to survey your current Christian neighborhood prayerfully may lead to unnecessary frustration. Some do so because they are not quite ready to think of marriage, possibly for economic reasons. But solving the problem of a marriage decision and getting married are two different things. It is a great relief to have the spouse in the bag as it were, and both of you merely waiting for the fullness of time to consummate the union.

CONCLUSION

We may conclude this all-important section by saying that one's "convictions"—inward witness- must remain the bedrock of a marriage partner's choice. Other considerations must play a secondary part, serving only to buttress the conviction. Because convictions are from the Lord, they embody God's expectations concerning our goals and mission in life. They also represent strengths and weaknesses that complement each other for purposes of stability. Therefore, we must be paired with only those with whom we can achieve our individual goals to the best of our abilities.

To appreciate this, let us imagine a situation where a young man is emotionally attracted to Miss A, even before he has a chance to pray about it. He "shadows" Miss A as it were, and further discovers that he likes her. All this time, Miss A is not aware of his intentions and treats him with courtesy and friendliness. Let us suppose he then goes to pray and finds that the inward witness about Miss A is contrary to his feelings. If anything, the Lord appears to be saying that he should leave Miss A alone. With such clear convictions, it would be foolhardy to entertain any serious thoughts about Miss A, despite how he feels about her. All this is without prejudice to how Miss A will respond were he to propose.

Let us reverse the situation. Suppose it is the other way round. A young man receives an inward witness about Miss B but finds that he hardly knows her. He again "shadows" her as it were, and finds that he does not know or like her, not spontaneously. He could see occasional flashes that draw him, but nothing much. He returns to the Lord with his reservations and finds that his convictions are stronger, contrary to his feelings. He must then ask the Lord to prepare him for that relationship so that it can develop naturally. He will soon discover on further scrutiny, that his feelings have started to change, enough to make a proposal imminent. All this is without prejudice to the response he will get when he goes to make his proposal.

Let us take another example. A young lady may find that Mr. X has been particularly lovely to her of late. She did not mind Mr. X's company and was wondering what his intentions were. On the other hand, Mr. X had no intention to start with but was being friendly, or so he thought. She may find that on waiting on the Lord, what had begun as a feeling has acquired an inward witness. One day, Mr. X turns up with a proposal because he had fallen in love while trying to be friendly and had a definite conviction. The young lady knew very little about Mr. X. But after she started to pray, she also decided to look a bit more closely. All she found were prospects and potentials, but nothing tangible to inspire her. She saw a great deal of struggle ahead, and possibly some suffering too. As a result, she decides to give Mr. X a cold response, neither no, nor yes.

To turn down a proposal for marriage for which you have conviction, because of a seemingly depressing economic prospect, for example, may prove a regrettable error. The apostle Paul by the Holy Ghost declared in 2 Corinthians 5:7: "For we walk by faith, not by sight." In other words, we go by what the Holy Spirit tells us, not by what we see. What we see now, which is not in line with what the Holy Spirit is telling us will give way, and what the Holy Spirit is telling us which we do not see, will come to be. This is what creative faith is all about. "Calling those things that be not as though they were" (Romans 4:17).

We often speak glibly about the triumph of faith. We fail to recognize that victory implies a battle that was fought and won or a struggle fought and won. Where there are no battles, there would be no victories and no defeats.

WHERE THERE ARE DIFFICULTIES?

Several young men and women may be wondering today why Mr. Right or Miss Right is yet to come along. A young man expressed his frustrations to me: "All the people I want to marry don't want to marry me: all the ones who are willing to marry me, I don't want to marry." When a young lady spoke to me recently, she complained of getting proposals from unmarriageable people, either because of the crucial spiritual orientation or other considerations. Some years ago, I was privileged to share with a gentleman rather intimately, about his persisting state of bachelorhood. He told me he had been quite open, but still had not found a match. I asked him if he was sure that he was quite open. He said he was as open as he possibly could be on a matter like this. I asked him if he felt he could afford to be open before the Lord. He wasn't too sure about that.

What does it mean to be open? I know several people who have told me that there was no way they could be that open. That would imply being non-selective, and since marriage is a matter of choice, it has to be selective.

There is a way we can practice the highest degree of openness possible under the circumstances. It is a way I wholeheartedly recommend because, in the final analysis, it opened the way for my wife and me to meet. Here it is!

If one were to go to the Lord and say: "Lord, I will marry anybody at all, on one and one condition alone; that You approve of the person as the right choice for me," the individual would have opened the door as wide as it ever can be under the circumstances. This prayer implies that you stand a chance to marry anybody or be married to anybody hypothetically. This kind of openness is quite similar to the open-ended prayer of Abraham's servant spoken of earlier.

Some would argue that giving everybody a chance as it were is quite unrealistic. Some ladies have told me that they do not bother to pray about some of the proposals they receive. Suffice it to say that those who open up to the Lord with humility will find that the path to happiness in marriage will come sooner than they could have imagined.

One must emphasize, though, that there is a clear distinction between being open to marrying any prospective suitor or marriage partner and being fully open before the Lord. When one is open before the Lord, a potential suitor may not necessarily know anything about it, neither would a prospective bride.

Therefore, being fully open in this sense would mean considering every eligible person in one's "Christian neighborhood," whom the Lord has brought across your path of life. It does not mean making proposals to these people, nor does it mean accepting their proposals. No. It means prayerfully considering each one before the Lord so that you do not miss the crucial Miss Right, or Mr. Right because you did not bother to ask the Lord when your paths crossed in your "Christian neighborhood." I believe this is the most sensible position to adopt under the circumstances for every Christian young man or lady who desires God's perfect will in marriage.

Those who have put this principle into practice realize sooner than later that the path to the altar where they would have the golden chance to kiss their bride or be kissed by their groom is not after all as long as they thought it would be.

4

PROPOSALS AND RESPONSES

Whoso findeth a wife findeth a good thing, and obtaineth favour of the LORD (Proverbs 18:22).

This Bible passage puts the responsibility of finding a marriage partner on the man. “Whoso findeth a wife, findeth a good thing.” The implication is that the man is to go out there, court a lady, and marry her. He is to come to the lady with a convincing marriage proposal. A young lady said to me once: "The problem is that these young men don't know what they want these days. When they come here, they tell all kinds of stories, often stories that are so open-ended that you are left to wonder what on earth they are saying. They make insinuations that carry no commitment." I believe we have a lot to learn from Abraham's servant in Genesis 24. It is evident from his response after meeting Rebekah (Genesis 24:27) that she was a favour from the Lord.

Empowered by his conviction and the clear guiding hand of Almighty God, Abraham's servant, proceeded with a definite proposal. He could not even wait to do it.

And there was set meat before him to eat: but he said, I WILL NOT EAT UNTIL 1 HAVE TOLD MINE ERRAND. And he said, speak on. And he said, I am Abraham's servant.
—Genesis 24:33-34

Abraham's servant proceeded to tell Rebekah's family about the oath that his master made him swear, to the end that his son Isaac must marry from his father's family. Then he told them about his specific prayer to the Lord, during which he chose a recognition signal, something that God would use to point out to him the particular woman Isaac was to marry. He retold how Rebekah soon appeared and confirmed that she was the lady for Isaac by responding to him without prepping according to his prayers.

By doing this, he made it clear to Rebekah's family that his choice of the young lady was not only based on her physical beauty and great humility and grace but also on what he believes is God's will in marriage for Isaac.

Having declared his convictions and intention, he threw the ball straight into the court of Rebekah and her relations. He was saying to them: "This is our intention towards your daughter and sister. We want her to be Isaac's wife. Please answer one way or the other."

And now if you will deal kindly and truly with my master, tell me; that I may turn to the right hand, or to the left".
—Genesis 24:49

Despite his convictions and the vividness of God's direction and intervention, Abraham's servant was still fully aware that it does take two to marry. He said to them: "And now if you will deal kindly with my master, tell me; that I may turn to the right hand, or to the left." In other words, he said: "I recognize that it takes two to marry. So if despite all that I have told you, you still are not convinced enough to let Rebekah come with us, then tell me clearly so that I can continue my search."

We must take note of the fact that he did not impose his convictions on them. He only used them, and how he came about them, to buttress his proposal. He left Rebekah and her people to make up their minds themselves.

When he ended his proposal, he left Rebekah, and her people in no doubt as to his clear intentions towards Rebekah, on behalf of Isaac.

Some time ago, a young man came to me with a series of revelations that convinced him that he should approach a particular Miss A and ask for her hand in marriage. I told him plainly: "When you do get to Miss A, make sure you tell her this story just like you have told it here. What that will do for you is that after you've gone. Miss A will be in no doubt as

to why you came."

When I saw him much later, he told me that their courtship had begun. I was not surprised.

Later on, I was privileged to meet the lady involved in this romance. I told her I was impressed by the honesty she reflected in her answer. I was proud of her for not playing the proverbial daughter of Eve. I wondered how she was able to be so decisive.

Her reply was most revealing. She told me how she was impressed by the nan's story of how the Lord spoke to him. It was so convincing that she had no difficulties hearing from the Lord when she prayed.

His story contained an impressive conviction that a woman can lean on for support in times of doubt.

Marriage is mostly like sailing on an uncharted sea, and such a journey requires faith and love as anchors. Conviction is the rudder that steadies the boat when it rocks to the right hand or the left. Those who have it and know it, and stand on it, position themselves to give spiritual direction to the emerging union.

This straight-talk approach is the sense in which a marriage proposal is an early demonstration of leadership potential in the man. It is particularly so from a Christian perspective because the Bible says that the man is the head of the woman (1 Corinthians 11:3). Therefore, a proposal is one way a man can give a woman an idea of what kind of leader she is getting. Will he be a vacillatory head, who is unsure of himself, unsure of what he wants; unsure where God is leading him, and in which direction they will be going as a family. Will he be panicky under pressure, sly, undependable, diffident, uninspiring? Or will he be decisive, confident, dignified, loving, and gentle, always armed with a little touch of tenderness, someone who inspires followership naturally, someone who will lead the whole family daily to God?

There is also a sense in which a proposal has to do with honesty. Instead, some young men will hold on to a lady with almost oppressive attention, suggesting that they have hidden intentions by every gesture. The lady is left wondering when he would be ready to reveal his intentions. He comes along with insinuations and obscure comments that are supposedly laden with meaning. They show either his lack of conviction or his indecision or a lack of commitment to his conviction.

It is unfair to continue to closet a lady of marriageable age with such "worthless" attention under such circumstances.

In Matthew 5:37, we read:

But let your communication be, Yea, yea; Nay, nay: for whatsoever is more than these cometh of evil. (KJV)

Some Bible teachers believe, and possibly teach, that young men and women should be allowed to mix very freely. Much as I agree with this in part, I have seen that when they are all of marriageable age, they must be careful about forging several close relationships at the same time. Suppose a young man, who is old enough to marry, visits a particular sister also of marriageable age alone frequently: His attention will be sending a message to the lady in question and other members of the fellowship that he has intentions towards her. If the same kind of message is being sent in all directions all around, the chances are that no lady in that fellowship will take him seriously.

In Christian fellowship groups, where this caution is not in place, the result will be stress and strain amongst the young men and women, which may constitute an unwanted distraction that hurts the people's spiritual health. It usually results in a situation where several ladies may be confused about a particular young man's intention. It could also be the reverse situation where several young men wait for an answer from a specific lady.

Let us take a cue from Abraham's servant. A young man proposing to a lady should, therefore, observe some two golden rules:

- Be sure yourself, of precisely what you have come to say.

- Make your proposal to the lady in such a way that you leave a clear message. That message must speak about your love for her and your intention to seek her hand in marriage.

If there are useful elements of how you came by your conviction, telling the lady the details should prove helpful.

SHIFTING CONVICTIONS

Sometimes, it would appear that the young men are not fully aware of the implications of a conviction and what it can do to the individual's credibility as a Christian.

A young lady once said to me, "I don't think very much of his convictions. He has had several that I know of, and the interval between some of them are so short that you naturally wonder where they are coming from."

One must avoid a hasty proposal that reflects the pressure to get there before someone else does. The result is a carnal situation that could be as confusing as it is dangerous to the spiritual and emotional health of one or both of the people involved.

The sneer about "shifting convictions" can only bother someone who was not honest about his convictions.

The Psalmist said in Psalm 26:1;

"Judge me, O LORD, for I have walked in my integrity... "

Once I am sure that I have neither lied to myself nor anybody about my convictions and love and that I have stated them both the way they were, I would take the sneers as they come and take my case to the Lord like the Prophet Jeremiah, where he said:

O LORD, thou knowest: remember me and visit me and revenge me of my persecutors; take me not away in thy longsuffering: KNOW THAT FOR THY SAKE I HAVE SUFFERED REBUKE.

Thy words were found, and I did eat them: and thy word was unto me the joy and rejoicing of mine heart: for I am called by thy name, O LORD God of hosts.
—Jeremiah 15:15-16

STAYING WITH YOUR CONVICTION

Abraham's servant was quite willing to try somewhere else if Rebekah and her people answered him otherwise. And this was despite his deep convictions. He was ready to take that chance, confident that the LORD who had led him that far, would lead him to the very end. A person with a similar conviction must then patiently wait for the Lord to work things out to the end.

A poster says: "Love is like the five loaves and the two fishes," (that the little lad gave to Jesus to feed the five thousand). "It is not worth much until you give it away." And I dare say that those who give theirs away will find that the eternal law of sowing and reaping (Genesis 8:22, Galatians 6:7) will begin to operate.

Some ladies may present an intimidating, haughty facade that can turn a young man away. But that is not to say that a proposal would be turned down outright by them. This perseverance despite the discouraging façade is the power of a love that has a conviction. The most tragic thing that I have heard is a gentleman who couldn't believe years later that a certain lady could have accepted him years before. The way he saw her then, it was like, "Go and look for people who would give you some attention, please. Don't hang your coat where the elephants hang theirs." By the time they met again, 'the die was cast' for the two of them. They may both be enjoying second best relationships.

BATTERED CONFIDENCE

A young man proposing may sound hedgy, hesitant or unsure because he was badly rebuffed the last time he tried to propose to a lady. After that experience, he decided to protect his ego somewhat in the future. This hedging is a well-known phenomenon. His previous outing dealt a deadly blow to his self-confidence and spiritual orientation that he was not ready for a second experience.

The Prophet Isaiah has these words of sympathy:

Who is among you that feareth the LORD, that obeyeth the voice of his servant, that walketh in darkness, and hath no light? Let him trust in the name of the LORD, and stay upon his God.
—Isaiah 50:10

A young man said that is why he does not mention God in his proposals. He goes there to say, "'I love you, dear, will you marry me?' I can't stand all that talk of lying with God's name. If they say: 'Sorry, no,' I will walk away."

I have heard this kind of argument before concerning convictions. In fact, in one church where I was speaking on the subject, "Hearing from God," one young man got up during question time to say: "I never say that God told me, or that God said. I will tell you what I think," or words to that effect.

I have heard complaints from young ladies that some young men use God's name to intimidate them. Some of the young men, they say, give the impression that if you do not say yes to them, then you would be disobeying God.

Marrying because you fear to disobey God when the conviction is not yours, but someone else's is like entering a self-imposed prison yard. A young lady has adequate protection from proposals like that, and we shall go into it in detail when we look at the principles that guide responses to a marriage proposal.

HANDLING RESPONSES

Whoso findeth a wife, findeth a good thing, and obtaineth favour of the Lord. (Proverbs 18:22)

There is a sense in which a lady is waiting for the man who will come and find her, and consider her a favour from the Lord, just as Abraham's servant found Rebekah for Isaac.

It is not surprising, therefore, that Rebekah responded the way she did. She only had a few hours to make up her mind.

Her relations were first with their response. They, too, were convinced. They also saw the hand of the Lord clearly in the events that were unfolding.

Behold, Rebekah is before thee, take her and go, and let her be thy master's son's wife, AS THE LORD HATH SPOKEN.
—Genesis 24:5

With this response in his hand, the servant of Abraham moved quickly to seal the commitment. Rebekah had less than twelve hours to decide.

And they did eat and drink, he and the men that were with him, and tarried all night; and they rose in the morning, and he said, Send me away unto my master.

And her brother and her mother said, Let the damsel abide with us a few days, at the least ten; after that, she shall go.

And he said unto them, Hinder me not, seeing the LORD hath prospered my way; send me away that I may go to my master.

And they said. We would call the damsel and inquire at her mouth.

—Genesis 24:54-57 (KJV)

Rebekah must have been impressed by the gentleman's conviction that this is the will of God. Abraham's servant stated and restated it, making it the pivot of his push to set aside ceremonial delays. Rebekah's relations must have felt that Rebekah would resolve the matter very quickly. "Surely, she wouldn't be that eager to leave home, would she?" They must have wondered to themselves. "She would be able to help us save face, and at least give the impression that she is not overly carried away by the prospects of the marriage." They were disappointed.

And they called Rebekah, and said unto her, Wilt thou go with this man? And she said I WILL GO.

And they sent away Rebekah their sister, and her nurse, and Abraham's servant, and his men.

—Genesis 24:58-59 (KJV)

There may be ladies who would say, "But that is not my problem. My problem is that nobody has come to say anything lately."

This kind of situation is a fact of life, I suppose. Some ladies turn down suitors by the day. Others wait a long time before someone will turn up.

I believe that the Lord has a way of taking care of this in the lives of His people. As the saying goes, "Every dog has his day."

During a recent discussion, one lady said to me: "I believe the ladies also need a good orientation on this. Bringing your life to a halt because you are waiting to be found by someone is just not acceptable. It could lead to a great deal of agonizing frustration for the women."

I can very readily identify with that point of view because I believe in active rather than passive waiting on the Lord. Indeed the Bible says, "They that wait upon the Lord shall renew their strength." (Isaiah 40:31). That in no way suggests paralysis, nor suspended animation. Waiting should involve communion that should direct activity and orientation, and channel our energies to productive areas of the Christian life, like various forms of witnessing activities.

From what we have said already, it is evident that a lady cannot marry everyone, nor just anyone. The same considerations that apply to the man also apply to the woman. She needs to be fully persuaded about the will of God; she needs to have some feelings for the gentleman before she can accept the proposal.

Sometimes, some ladies do not handle their responses well, particularly those who feel somewhat "oppressed" by these attentions that they do not appreciate.

One young lady said to me: "Believe me, I try to be as nice as I can, but sometimes you just can't help yourself."

PROBLEMS WITH PROPOSALS AND RESPONSES

Having a humble spirit before the Lord will go a long way to galvanize our faith and get the answer that we desire coming down to us when dealing with this matter of proposals and responses. Someone with a humble spirit will pray a prayer like this:

"Lord, please lead me to whoever you want me to marry.

Help me to recognize him or her whenever and wherever we meet. Please help me to love him or her, and help me to be faithful too."

Having offered a prayer like the one above, one can confidently leave the matter in the hands of the Lord, watching out for those signals that denote the direction of the divine will. An open disposition while watching and waiting is a great asset. In His goodness, the Lord will guide the believer's footsteps to the right person for him or her.

By presenting a humble spirit, we would neither despise nor deride anybody nor scorn their approaches. Even where we are not convinced about it, we would still politely tell them that we are not convinced, and prayerfully urge them to continue their search elsewhere. As we do this, the Lord will be pleased with the way we are reflecting the life of Christ, who is the Light of the world, to our generation, and will bless us as a result, by sending us our dream wife or husband.

A gentleman or lady walking in this way, with a humble spirit before the Lord, has a right to believe that, wherever his dream wife or husband is, the Lord will find him or her and cause their paths to cross to His glory.

But when our attitude reflects pride, when we despise the people of God, when we are inconsiderate to our brother or sister, then the eternal law of sowing and reaping will overtake us, and things will begin to run out of hand for us in this area.

This approach was the point the apostle Peter was making when he wrote about "faith additives."

And beside this, giving all diligence, add to your faith virtue; and to virtue knowledge; And to knowledge temperance; and to temperance patience; and to patience godliness; And to godliness brotherly kindness; and to brotherly kindness charity
—2 Peter 1:5-7 (KJV)

He also wrote about what we gain and the consequences we suffer when we ignore these virtues or "faith additives" in 2 Peter 1:8-11.

For if these things be in you, and abound, they make you that you shall neither be barren nor unfruitful in the knowledge of our Lord Jesus Christ. But he that lacketh these things is blind, and cannot see afar off, and hath forgotten that he was purged from his old sins.

Wherefore the rather, brethren, give diligence to make your calling and election sure, for if you do these things, ye shall never fall: For so an entrance shall be ministered unto you abundantly into the everlasting Kingdom of our Lord and Saviour Jesus Christ. (KJV)

CONFLICTING RESPONSES

A young man once said to me: "Everything she does or says to me, confirms my convictions. But when I put the question pointedly to her, she turns me down." When he could not get a positive answer from her after about a year or more, I advised the young man to stick to what the lady was saying and forget her insinuations. I advised him to look somewhere else.

I believe that we should do our best to be consistent Christians in everything we say or do. Stringing a man along, encouraging him, to hold on to him, just in case no one else turns up, is to say the very least unfair.

A young man should be able to take a sister's no, as no unless he has any other reason to imagine that the sister's ordinary speech is now some sort of tongues that require interpretation. However, I must add that the ladies being naturally coy may prefer the legal maxim "*Qui tacit consentire*" to prevail, i.e., silence denotes consent. I don't remember my wife responding to my proposal in many words that fateful evening in 1975 until she said a very impressive and firm "I do" at the altar in 1978.

Sometimes a sister may claim that God has not said anything yet. This so-called "unwillingness of God to say anything" may last for months, if not years. The duration makes you wonder whether they now have long vacations in heaven.

However, we must admit that some people need time to sort out their emotions from their convictions. A sister may sense some inner peace about a proposed relationship but on serious thought, find that she needs some time to sort out her feelings because she hardly knows the individual concerned. The brother should be able to appreciate that and try and woo the lady patiently.

I must emphasize the need for patience. Some young men tend to jump around the whole place, making proposals. Each time they don't get a quick-fix answer, they just bounce off like a tennis ball. One young lady in a particular city told me how she was hurt by one of these "bouncy brothers." Bouncing around like that is a sign of fickleness and an element of immaturity. Going in and out of relationships with ease would also worry a prospective wife. "If he has this trait, might it not resurface after the wedding?" Such attitudes reinforce fears and doubts, rather than help build faith and trust between two people from different backgrounds.

THE TRAUMA OF REJECTION

One of the most tormenting emotional traumas is unrequited love. This is why it is quite crucial to indicate your interest or lack of it in a proposal as early as possible, and be as firm and as friendly about it as you possibly can. I doubt that anyone is so blind as not to notice that what started as a casual platonic friendship of two brethren is beginning to develop expectations at one or the other end, And having seen that, it would be unfair to continue to relate as if nothing has changed. Someone is bound to get hurt that way.

The wise thing to do is reduce contact and assist the other party in curing their "lovingitis." That way, they will come to appreciate and respect you, no matter what happens.

Having traumatizing experiences trying to engage does not mean that the individual should fold up the idea and tuck it away. A young man in his mid-thirties told me he didn't care much anymore. I asked him if he had a vow of celibacy. He said, "No." I said, "Well, remember that you have to go out there and find a wife."

We have shared some things here that should help a young man be decisive and convincing like Abraham's servant when seeking to be engaged to a lady. But if the girls still turn you down despite everything you have done, you should quietly continue to seek the Lord and search for that lady with whom the Lord will have you build your home. But to keep it totally out of focus will be like denial. We must continue like Abraham, by not staggering at the promises of God through unbelief.

And being not weak in faith, - He staggered not at the promise of God through unbelief; but was strong in faith, giving glory to God. And being fully persuaded that, what He had promised, He was able also to perform.

And therefore it was imputed unto him for righteousness

—Romans 4:19-22 (KJV)

DECEITFUL WAYS OF CHOICE AND RESPONSES

Testimonies have emerged about what we may call "wolves in sheep's clothing," people who come into the fold pretending to be born again, to carry a brother or a sister away. They are very loud with their Amens, and their shouts of Hallelujah.

Let me say right away that pretensions would hardly fool a Christian young man or woman who is very sincere about following the Lord. And even where they are, the Lord has a way of revealing the exact position of things before the individual commits a permanent error. When we are sincere before the Lord in this area of our lives, we can count on the LORD to see us through. For a born-again Christian to fall prey to a deceiver, it must likely be because they discarded the clear and direct Word of the Lord to them. The pressure of time and circumstance may have caused them to buckle.

The Lord has His way of rewarding those who pretend to be what they are not to trap a child of God. Once upon a time, there was a couple who learned this lesson the hard way. The gentleman entered the fellowship ostensibly to catch a bride from the fold. Unknown to him, the lady also joined with the same objective. They met, courted, and married. After the wedding, it dawned on both of them that they are victims of their plots. "I can't imagine you behaving like this. I thought you were a Christian," one of them blurted out in the middle of an altercation. "Same here too," the other replied. "I thought I was marrying a Christian." That was the crisis flashpoint that forced them to true repentance and salvation.

Also, employing the world's ways to catch a man or woman to be your husband or wife can be quite disastrous, and maybe a tell-tale sign that the seductive individual is under the spell of an unclean spirit or a seducing spirit. As one brother rightly put it, "If you catch your wife or husband using seductive tactics, then you have opened them up to future seductions unwittingly, and you may end up reaping what you have sown. if you do not repent."

There is nothing as eternally rewarding as walking the straight and narrow path recommended by our Lord Jesus, rather than the broad way of the world. The Bible has a great deal to say about this.

And be not conformed to this world, but be ye transformed by the renewing of your mind, that you may prove what that good is, and acceptable, and perfect, will of God (Romans 12:2).

For to be carnally minded is death, but to be spiritually minded is life and peace. Because the carnal mind is enmity against God; for it is not subject to the law of God, neither indeed can be. So then they that are in the flesh cannot please God.
—Romans 8:6 – 8 (KJV)

The just shall live by faith. Dying to self, and the ways dictated by self and its pressures is the one way to release the power of the Holy Spirit of God locked up within us. The Bible tells us that God can do exceeding abundantly above all that we can ever ask or think (Ephesians 3:20). But it was careful to mention that He does so according to the power at work in us. Getting that power to work for us from within us continues to be the challenge before every believer. The one way to ensure that we get it to operate continually is by removing all obstacles of sin and self.

A WORD FOR THOSE WHO STILL WAIT

As I write this, my heart goes out to those faithful men and women who still wait. I have a word from the Lord for you. Perhaps, you have tried just about everything you know— fasted, prayed, been to deliverance sessions, breakthrough sessions, name it. Still, the husband or wife continues to elude you. Let me share with you this word that the Lord gave me.

"Favour will come to those who pursue the will of God, to the glory of God alone, in their lives." Try this today. Try and desire God's will for God's glory in this area of your life. Persist in this desire. Resist every effort to shift you from that position. As you pray, meditate along. Let your body, soul, and spirit blend together in that desire. Enter the presence of the Lord, and empty all self-worth before Him with joy. Insist on His will for His glory alone. After some time, help will come from heaven to you. Watch out for that help. It comes in usual and unusual ways through expected and unexpected sources, Amen— Glory Alleluia.

5

THE ENGAGEMENT

The engagement begins when the two people pledge their mutual love and belief that the Lord is leading them to become husband and wife. This mutual acceptance of each other is quite important because it marks the real onset of the relationship proper: the courtship. In some cultures, this is celebrated and formalized with the man giving an engagement ring to the prospective bride.

This engagement is quite different from the traditional engagement ceremony performed before the wedding in some cultures in Nigeria. The prospective couple will say a prayer of commitment to a future together with God.

This engagement rests squarely on commitment. I know a couple who were engaged continuously for nine years before they finally got married. They pledged a life together before the Lord and maintained that pledge for nine whole years by the grace of God.

A Christian should bring nothing less than total commitment to an engagement. Total commitment means that you will keep it to the end once you have given your word.

Ruth, the Moabitess, is a Biblical example of someone who brought an impressive degree of commitment to her marital relationship. Even after her husband died, she still clung to her mother-in-law with these words:

And Ruth said, Entreat me not to leave thee, or to return from following after thee: for wither thou goest, I will go; and where thou lodgest, I will lodge: thy people shall be my people, and thy God my God:

Where thou diest, will I die, and there will I be buried: the LORD do so to me, and more also, if aught but death part thee and me.
—Ruth 1:16-17 (KJV)

But someone may say: "Oh no, this is the sort of commitment you should bring to a marriage, not to an engagement." The truth is that if you do not have this sort of commitment during the engagement, then the marriage itself may never take place.

It bears repeating, a million times over, that engagements resulting from marriage proposals, made and accepted, must of necessity be born of conviction as to the mind of God and the love the two people share. Anything short of that will be building on the wrong foundation.

The operative word is commitment. The two parties must be committed to each other. This commitment is what is lacking in most of the relationships that break down. The two parties never brought the highest level of commitment to the engagement. You can predict the relationships that will break down by the degree of commitment reflected by the two parties.

When a young man acts in a way that sort of says: "Let us be going, and then we shall see how it will turn out," and the lady accepts that kind of proposal, then sooner or later, they will find reasons not to continue. There is no commitment to this type of marriage proposal. What the two parties have entered into is a trial relationship and not engagement. It is certainly not the kind of engagement that one would expect between two Christians.

Convictions must lead to commitment. Without commitment, engagements will continue to break down, and the family of God will be no different from the people of the world. The world does trial marriages. "Let's live together for a while. If it works, we formalize it. If it doesn't, we part without any hassle, no courts, no attorneys, no legal fees, no burdens."

I have seen a great deal of misery born of this failure to grasp the place of commitment to engagement among believers. A preacher said, "An engagement is as good as a marriage. You have committed yourself to an individual, and you should not go back on that commitment." He quoted Psalm 15, verse 4: "He that sweareth to his own hurt and changeth not."

Our Lord Jesus taught us in Matthew 5, verse 33 to 37, that we should not swear at all, but that our yes should be yes; And our no, no. Anything short of this is evil.

The Psalmist caught the true essence of commitment, where he said, "I have sworn, and I will perform it, that I will keep thy righteous judgments."

Under Joshua's leadership, the children of Israel learned that when you make a commitment in the name of the Lord, you alter it at your peril. A case in point was the clever deception by the Gibeonites. They used trickery to obtain a friendship treaty from the elders of Israel, who based their commitment on the presumption that the Gibeonites lived very far away. The Bible pointedly remarked in Joshua chapter 9, verses 14 and 15:

And the men took of their victuals and asked not counsel at the mouth of the LORD. And Joshua made peace with them, and made a league with them, to let them live: and the princes of the congregation sware unto them.

This Gibeonite treaty was even a commitment made in error under pretenses. Nevertheless, made it was and in the name of the Lord too.

And it came to pass at the end of three days after they had made a league with them, that they heard that they were their neighbors and that they dwelt among them.

And the children of Israel smote them not, because the princes of the congregation had sworn unto them by the LORD God of Israel. And all the congregation murmured against the princes. But all the princes said unto all the congregation, we have sworn unto them by the LORD God of Israel; now therefore we may not touch them.
—Joshua 9:16,18 and 19 (KJV)

Nobody should take any engagement they make in the name of the Lord lightly. Those who have no conviction and no commitment should steer clear of Christian engagement in the name of the Lord, to avoid possible repercussions. "The fear of the Lord is the beginning of wisdom. And the knowledge of the Holy One is understanding."

(Proverbs 9:10) Joshua and the elders of Israel revealed that they had that much spiritual sense. We Christians should show no less.

BROKEN ENGAGEMENTS

Despite all that we have said above, engagements do break down. The truth is that we are experiencing this now in fellowships here in Nigeria more than ever before. One could adduce a couple of reasons why this is so.

The very first one is simply a question of numbers. There certainly are many more Christians today in Nigeria than in the early seventies.

The Christians were also clustered in fewer fellowships with established counseling traditions to guide young people to the path of discipleship and total commitment to the Lord Jesus. Because the people are so many, effective follow-up programs for young Christians, designed to establish them in the ways of the Lord, are in short supply when compared to the need. And this has nothing to do with the concept of the "good old days."

The teaching that Christians are in the world but not of the world (John 17:15-16) was standard teaching in many young people's fellowships as an essential gospel. We discussed the practical implications of this earlier. All these discipleship efforts helped grow Christians who have a clear sense of what it means to be Christian. In 1 Corinthians chapter 15, verse 34, the apostle Paul laments the lack of knowledge of the Lord in his time.

Awake to righteousness, and sin not; for some have not the knowledge of God: I speak this to your shame.

IN LOVE AND OUT OF LOVE

It is not too difficult to see why an engagement can fall apart. If all the people did was "fall in love," without any conviction, courtship may turn up reasons why they should fall out of love. A conviction that inward witness stabilizes a relationship and always acts as a guiding star after the engagement.

Each time I am dealing with young people whose engagements have fallen apart, I want to ask them: "How did it all start, and who decided it should be? Was it you alone, or did you have any conviction from the Spirit of the LORD? What is your testimony of this relationship that is about to fall apart? Did it start in the flesh or the Spirit?"

They will need to go back to the very beginning, to be able to understand what is happening to them on the way.

Some of our young people became victims of "the crown without the cross" philosophy. The fact that abundant life exists in Christ (John 10:10) does not reduce the responsibility we have to work out our salvation daily with fear and trembling (Philippians 2:12). Successful marriages do not reflect the absence of challenges of humility, love, sacrifice, understanding, and the like. Instead, it demonstrates the capacity to tap these attributes of God into our lives and reflect them in our relationships.

CARRY-OVER RELATIONSHIPS

As the name suggests, a "carry-over relationship" began before the two people were born again, and continued afterward. Some people wondered whether the relationship should not break up since God's purposes were not considered when it began. This urge to disband is particularly so if the relationship itself had a great deal of "illicit" sexual gratification. A sense of disgust would naturally result after being convicted of their sins and taking steps to repent. The two people would often drift apart naturally, to avoid the trap of a cycle of continuing sexual immorality.

Parting ways under this kind of circumstance, at least for a good while, would be a wise thing to do, as old passions have a way of flaring up again and again if the two people continue to see each other closely and exclusively. T*he Bible says that we are not ignorant of the devil's tricks or devices (2 Corinthians 2:11).*

However, it is quite possible that an existing "carry-over relationship" may have something to do with God's purposes in the lives of the two people. I once heard of a very close relationship that broke up because the two people felt called of the Lord in different directions. They could not see a meeting point in the visions they had of the call of God on their lives individually.

Under such circumstances, the relationship's break-up should always be cordial, as the resolve was mutual.

However, we must admit that some carry-over relationships may still stand up to the glare of heavenly scrutiny. This possibility is why the individuals must always seek counsel from the Lord and resist the temptation to be presumptuous or legalistic.

SOWING AND REAPING

Some have gone ahead to contract relationships that they knew were not of the Lord. They are often pressure-driven, emotional, chronological, or pressure from well-meaning friends and relations. Under such circumstances, it would be a matter of time before the cleavages appear on several lines of incompatibility, spiritual and psychological. Besides, since it is the "I," rather than the LORD, responsible for the decision to go ahead and contract the relationship, a spiritually sensitive believer will soon feel that inevitable condemnation in his or her heart any child of God knows only too well. He or she will then suffer such a significant loss of confidence each time they contemplate going ahead with plans to consummate the union because of the condemnation he or she always senses within.

And hereby we know that we are of the truth, and shall assure our hearts before him. For if our heart condemn us. God is greater than our heart and knoweth all things. Beloved, if our heart condemn us not, then have we confidence toward God. And whatsoever we ask, we receive of him, because we keep his commandments, and do those things that are pleasing in his sight.

—1 John 3:19-22 (KJV)

The cancellation or annulment of this kind of relationship, which inevitably follows, is often compelled by developing realities that give a foretaste of the immediate future. Without a conviction, the Christian soon discovers that the prayer of faith to change adverse situations is impossible since the error was willful. This willful disobedience was the point that the Apostle Paul made in 2 Corinthians chapter 10, verse 4 to 6:

For the weapons of our warfare are not carnal, but mighty through God to the pulling down of strongholds: Casting down imaginations, and every high thing that exalteth itself against the knowledge of God, and bringing into captivity every thought to the obedience of Christ, and having in a readiness to revenge all disobedience, when your obedience is fulfilled.

Without obedience, spiritual weapons prove ineffective. Spiritual weapons derive their potency from the Lord, and they are galvanized into action by our obedience to specific things the Lord spoke to us, in our hearts, or by His word.

We may avoid this kind of spiritual incapacitation through genuine repentance. Once there is sincere repentance, God's grace will be restored in that area of the individual's life, enabling him or her to have faith to believe the Lord for a genuine breakthrough. Withdrawing from the relationship and the will to do so must be seen as part of the Lord's grace and mercy.

THE INEVITABLE BREAKDOWN

In the absence of grace, some breakdowns are inevitable. This breakdown has to do with immorality and so-called flirtatious tendencies. These gnaw at the mutual trust between the two people, which is at the heart of the relationship. If one party to a marriage engagement is known to move here, there and yonder, with testimonies that are unbecoming of a Christian, they will need to change their ways to restore trust.

Most people will politely excuse themselves from a relationship like that since they invariably raise several fundamental questions. The first one has to do with whether the party involved in immoral behavior has genuinely been born again, or whether the sin is a one-off.

But fornication, and all uncleanness, or covetousness, let it not be once named among you, as becometh saints; Neither filthiness, nor foolish

talking, nor jesting, which are not convenient; but rather giving of thanks.
—Ephesians 5:3-4 (KJV)

Brethren if a man be overtaken in a fault, ye which are spiritual, restore such an one in the Spirit of meekness; considering thyself, lest thou also be tempted
—Galatians 6:1 (KJV)

If the individual involved was indeed overtaken in a fault and is genuinely penitent, the brother or sister should forgive, in line with God's word. The Lord will give the enabling grace for inner healing to occur.

Take heed to yourselves; if thy brother trespass against thee, rebuke him; and if he repents forgive him.

And if he trespass against thee seven times in a day, and seven times in a day turn again to thee, saying, I repent; thou shall forgive him. And the disciples said unto the Lord, Increase our faith.
—Luke 17:3-4 (KJV)

From the disciples' response, asking the Lord to increase their faith, we can see that what is involved is not that easy. Therefore, nobody should pressure another person to accept a relationship where there has been such a breach of trust, particularly at this early stage. If you forgive and take back the relationship, it should be because you were convinced of the Holy Spirit to do so, not necessarily because Brother A or Sister B said so.

This personal decision is crucial because you are the one who will live with the person who breached the trust between you. You will need that increase in faith that the disciples were asking for to weather through. Accept the relationship without asking the Lord for inner healing, and you may find yourself going through your married life with this chronic suspicion that this trust can be breached again, or is probably on-going without your knowing. That will be very destructive in many ways, with the stress and tendency to high blood pressure associated with chronic stress.

I was privileged to share the experience of a fine Christian gentleman so many years ago. He was still single then and engaged to marry a certain lady who lived in the northern part of Nigeria. He had bizarre revelations of the result of that union. Many of them involved severe spiritual struggles in the heavenly realms.

When we prayed about this, the Lord revealed that He was telling him what the relationship would entail for him. Since he was victorious each time, he could take on the spiritual struggle that the relationship would entail. The Lord added something quite interesting. He said the gentleman could pass-up the relationship if he didn't feel like taking it on. It was his decision. I asked him what he would do. He said he would talk to the Lord about it. I was not surprised that he passed-up the relationship.

But if your fiance or fiancee is suffering from "sexual incontinence," then it might be better to take him or her for deliverance and a discipleship program first before you re-consider what steps you need to take further. If they are unwilling to go, that will be a strong indication that they do not want the relationship to **continue.**

BREAKING POINT

There must be a time in some relationships when the inevitable will finally become a reality. But just before the individual calls it all off, it would be good to have a very honest re-assessment before the Lord, and truthfully answer some direct questions.

- I hope this break is not because I have seen someone else I feel I like better.

- I hope I am not doing what the Lord has not allowed in my life. This will be despite justifiable reasons that informed my decision, and which brought about the impasse.

Many Christians will agree that if a relationship must break, it is better to fail at this stage. This break will forestall the moral burden that will arise for the individuals if things deteriorate irredeemably at a later stage; after the wedding.

The only question that will remain after a break of a relationship that started with conviction and love is where to assign the blame. Will it be better to attribute the failure to inadequate or incorrect communication, in which case the conviction was not a conviction, or is the fault primarily in the individuals' inability to conform to God's word that stresses love and godliness?

This retrospective analysis is not easy for the individual who was deeply sincere when the relationship started. The Apostle Paul's admonition in Philippians chapter 3, verses 13 to 14, is quite instructive.

Brethren, I count not myself to have apprehended: but this one thing I do, forgetting those things which are behind, and reaching forth unto those things which are before,

I press toward the mark for the prize of the high calling of God in Christ Jesus.

All an individual may be able to say in prayer to the Lord is something like this: "Dear Lord, whatever may have been the problem here, please continue to lead and guide me, and make Your ways clear before me, in Jesus' name."

Sometimes, the Lord will reveal what went wrong. At other times. He may choose to ask us to move on in our walk with Him, forgetting those things that are behind. Since our lives and the experiences we pass through only make full meaning from an eternal perspective, there would be no need to dwell and brood unduly over incidents like this. After all, the Bible has said:

The secret things belong unto the LORD our God: but those things which are revealed belong unto us and to 'our children forever, that we may do all the words of this law.
—Deuteronomy 29:29

However, there is one good reason to try and prayerfully find out from the Lord what went wrong. This info is to assist us in avoiding such mistakes in the future. Convictions impart the mind of God to us. Our obedience to the principles of walking with the Lord ensures for us that we attain the revealed objectives.

SEEKING COUNSEL

"No man is an island unto himself," so the saying goes. In our local church here in Nigeria, engaged couples let the senior pastor know soon afterward. This connection will lead to their referral to an on-going series of 13 lectures designed for intending couples. There are many testimonies about the positive impact of this program. The claim is that separation and divorce are rare amongst those who went through it.

A great deal of counseling designed to assist engaged couples to work through difficulties and thorny issues does go on in many churches, and young people are always encouraged to avail themselves of the wise counsel of Christian elders in their local congregations or elsewhere.

The taste of the pudding is in the eating, so goes another saying. Marriage does take two, and integration is a significant challenge. The couple should get to know each other better before the wedding. It is a useful precaution to reduce the tension after the wedding. Those in cloud nine during courtship are soon brought down to earth after the wedding as they face the hard work of mutual love.

Sometimes it takes sharing of experiences to encourage an intending couple in a troubled relationship to persevere. The perception is that those who are happy today never had any challenges during their engagement and courtship. It is almost impossible to find a couple from two different backgrounds who did not find integration a challenge. With faith in God and a willingness to make changes, many happy couples came through their challenges. There is no magic to it. Happiness in marriage is hard work. Any happy team will testify to that.

THE BREAK

The break will occur when wounds run deep, and there is no healing of damaged bonds and no restoration of shattered confidences.

As regrettable as this may be, it may still be the best thing under the circumstances, for two people who now feel that starting the relationship in the first place was a colossal mistake. It would be better for them to pull apart and spare each other the terrible agony of a marriage relationship that has to be endured rather than enjoyed.

It is not unusual for either party to admit that they were experimenting, victims of the bandwagon effect. This bandwagon effect often arises when many friends get married, and the individual is under pressure not to be left behind. Accepting to enter the relationship was more to solve the problem posed by this psychological pressure than anything else.

But for those who cannot fathom what caused the break, the only reasonable thing to do is forget what is behind and move on. Stopping to brood and ruminate endlessly may lead to anger, frustration, and sometimes depression. One may say that these sentiments are inevitable under the circumstances. Yes, indeed, they are, but it is good to remember that they are both physically and spiritually harmful to the individual.

One thing that will always help when there is such a deep hurt is to ask the Lord for inner healing. The LORD GOD ALMIGHTY will surely make a way in that wilderness. There is "balm in Gilead" for the saints of the Lord.

TWO MISTAKES YOU CAN AVOID

- Never marry a person solely on another person's conviction.
- Do not marry a person you do not like not to talk of love.

I have encountered a few broken marriages not too long ago, that have made this warning inevitable. Some Christians suffering untold frustrations within their married life have blamed their misery on a particular prophecy they were assured, was a word from the Lord. I wholly acknowledge that God can help us through the counsel of others. But please ensure that the conviction at the very end of the day is yours. We all must learn to take full responsibility for the decisions we make in our lives. Other brothers, sisters, pastors, and counselors can only help us with principles in God's word and wisdom from spiritual maturity.

If people always push you here and there and yonder, ask the Holy Spirit to transform your will so that it will only yield to convictions coming from deep within you, or from your inner man. That is what walking in the Spirit is all about.

A man's understanding or intellect is transformed and streamlined by the Word of God. His feelings or emotions are constrained by the word of God and processed by the Holy Spirit. His will, on the other hand, should only surrender to the communion of the Holy Spirit.

6

COURTSHIP

There is a sense in which courtship implies discovery. It is essentially a period when two people engaged to marry discover each other to reduce early marriage friction.

One must be careful to state without equivocation that Christian courtship is not a time for the people to decide whether or not to marry each other. Christian courtship is for those who have discovered God's will for their lives. Also, they love each other and have decided to become husband and wife.

This definition is vitally important because some young men and women have acquired a reputation for breaking up engagements during courtship, for one reason or another. The problem that this creates for the individual is quite fundamental, and it borders on where precisely the decision-making center of his or her life lies. If Mr. A. says to Miss B, "I love you, and I believe it is God's will for us to get married," one would like to believe that Mr. A is fully aware of the implications of the contents of his proposal. If Miss B accepts the proposal and says: "I love you too, and having prayed, I believe it is the will of God for us to get married." One would also like to believe that she, too, fully appreciates the implications of her acceptance of the engagement proposal.

The essence of praying to the Lord to confirm or annul the choice of a marriage partner for the individual is to employ God's omniscience. To guarantee that the present and the future of the relationship will be in the individuals' best interests, not only in time but also in eternity.

God, who knows all about Miss B and Mr. A, their backgrounds and upbringing, expectations and ambitions, and their habits, useful or hurtful, have integrated their lives and decided that they stand a perfect chance of making each other happy. This means Mr. A and Miss B will make the best possible team for each of them, or an excellent team at the very least.

Whatever Mr. A discovers in Miss B during courtship, cannot, therefore, annul the engagement, since that attribute of Miss B has been known to the Almighty God in His omniscience, before leading them to engage each other. Not to accept that is to imply that God is less than Almighty and is not quite omniscient. This is why this issue is fundamental. The same goes for Miss B concerning Mr. A.

But then, someone may ask; "Suppose you discover something that you think you cannot accept in your wife or husband, what then are you supposed to do?"

I believe that there is no need to make this matter hypothetical. Let us take a practical example. Suppose Party A discovers that Party B is a very untidy person during courtship, with a less than acceptable degree of personal cleanliness. He or she may then decide that party B has unacceptable attributes, and as a result, calls off the engagement.

Indeed, Party A is concerned, at this present moment, with being tidy, and sees maintaining a high level of personal cleanliness as a *sine qua non* for marriage. If the other party does not have it, that should signal the end of the engagement.

Let us assume a situation where both are genuinely spiritual and have come to accept that each person has his or her flaws and that in leading them to make these choices, God knows that they can supplement and complement each other. As a result of this understanding, Party A would then proceed to assist party B in this area of weakness without criticism, but rather in the spirit of 1 Peter 4, verse 8, which says that love does cover a multitude of sins.

It is quite possible that years later, when the children have come, one discovers that you have to constantly pick-up after them to keep the house tidy. Party A would then realize that keeping things compulsively tidy may be an excellent idea, but is no longer such a matter of life and death that he or she thought it was. It is foolish to have broken such a smooth and enjoyable relationship in retrospect because those initial challenges are containable within the bounds of love.

Several young people go around with the impression that being a Christian implies that one must have no faults or weaknesses at all. There is a poster that is quite illuminating in this regard. It says something like this: "Please be patient with me, for God has not finished with me yet." This understanding implies that the work of perfection in us by the Holy Spirit is a continuing exercise and never really ends until we enter into eternity and His presence. To believe otherwise is not to give your partner room to continue to grow in the Lord.

A young man went to the Lord to complain that his courtship was not making any reasonable progress and had quickly deteriorated into debating sessions. Each party was determined to win the argument. He took his complaints to God in Church and hoped that the somber atmosphere of worship, coupled with the insight from the Holy Spirit given during the service, would serve to, at the very least, restore his battered expectations. He was not quite prepared for what he got at that evening service during the preacher's sermon.

Said the preacher: "Because of murmuring and complaining, a wilderness forty-day journey stretched to forty years for the

children of Israel."

He knew that sermon was not for the children of Israel. It was as if he heard the Lord clearly saying to him: "Look, if you don't stop all these complaints, then this period of friction, when one iron is sharpening another iron as it were, will become prolonged."

Iron sharpeneth iron; so a man sharpeneth the countenance of his friend.
—Proverbs 27:17 (KJV)

There is a question I often ask young people during my seminars: "What do you think you need most in a spouse?" The answers were typical of saints on their way to glory: "A partner that will serve the Lord with me forever."

As laudable as this answer may sound, I took the time to point out that they had not quite addressed the question. The reason is that knowing someone with whom you will serve the Lord faithfully now and in the future will require a proven gift of prophecy. The fact that someone is quite active in the service of the Lord today, though an excellent indication, is not foolproof. A professional colleague who is very busy in evangelism amongst the youth has never ceased to remind me that I used to feel, during our university days, that she would not survive. I know it was her perception since I never really said as much. There was no doubt that in the university fellowships of the seventies here in Nigeria, certain "giggly" dispositions were considered quite suspect. My friend is still very "giggly" even today.

I recall a gentleman who was quite active in the fellowship at the university in those days. I still remember a terminologically controversial testimony that he shared in those days, more because he raised eyebrows when he claimed to have "vomited sin." Many of his listeners wondered whether that was possible, but he felt they were treating a spiritually profound experience with disrespect. However, I had the opportunity of running into him in the city of Lagos, a year or two after he left the university. I asked him if he was still in fellowship with the Lord, and to which local Church he belonged. I was shocked when he admitted that he had very little time these days for such matters and could not settle down to fellowship with other Christians.

Someone like that with "profound" spiritual experiences may look a safe bet to a prospective marriage partner, anxious for a relationship that will prove useful to the Kingdom of God. But less than two years of life in the world as it were had blown all the fundamental lessons away. Undoubtedly one would need a proven gift of prophecy to have seen that.

BOAZ AND RUTH SHOW SOME WORTHY EXAMPLES

The book of Ruth in the Bible provides us with an example of how the individual should conduct a Christian courtship. Ruth had deep loyalty and commitment to her late husband's family. By following her mother-in-law's advice, she ended up in courtship with a kinsman, Boaz. Boaz himself was noticeably impressed by Ruth and had this to say of her:

And he said, Blessed be thou of the Lord, my daughter: for thou hast showed more kindness in the latter end than at the beginning, inasmuch as thou followedst not young men, whether poor or rich.

And now, my daughter, fear not; I will do to thee all that thou requires for all the city of my people doth know that thou art a virtuous woman.

And now, it is true that I am thy near kinsman: howbeit, there is a kinsman nearer than I.

Tarry this night, and it shall be in the morning, that if he will perform to thee the part of a kinsman, well; let him do the kinsman's part: but if he will not do the part of a kinsman to thee, then will I do the part of a kinsman to thee, as the Lord liveth: lie down until the morning

—Ruth 3:10-13

RUTH CHOOSES TO OBEY THE LORD

Ruth had the liberty to marry anyone in Judah or Israel. But the law required her to marry a kinsman. The kinsman had to be the very next of kin. To Ruth, it did not matter who this next of kin was, whether he was tall or short, ugly or beautiful, pleasant or unpleasant, young or old. She was confident that in opting to do things the way the Lord had prescribed them in the Law, God would certainly take care of her.

One must note that obeying the Lord always carries this risk of faith.

BOAZ—A MAN OF HONOUR

Boaz himself was also quite honorable. He was not going to take advantage of the familiarity between himself and Ruth, occasioned by Ruth's earlier contact with him during the wheat harvest, to deny the most direct next of kin what was his, by right. He had to wait to offer him the first right of refusal.

It is evident from the gentleman's answer (that is, the most direct next of kin) that Ruth would have regretted her decision had he agreed to take her on as a duty instead of Boaz, who held her in very high regard.

Then said Boaz, (to the next of kin) What day thou buyest the field in the hands of Naomi, thou must buy it also, of Ruth the Moabitess, the wife of the dead, to raise up the name of the dead upon his inheritance.

And the kinsman said, I cannot redeem it for myself, lest I mar my inheritance: redeem thou my right to thyself; for I cannot redeem it

—Ruth 4:5-6

Boaz demonstrated maturity, honor, and grace that is worth noting. A situation where a young man or woman "muscles" into an existing courtship because he or she is interested in one of the parties to the relationship, is to say the very least, entirely unacceptable if not downright detestable.

I recall a young man in Kano city, here in Nigeria, who called to make an engagement proposal to a lady. The lady waited to hear him out and politely told him that she was already in a relationship of sorts and was unavailable. The young man was naturally disheartened and confused. He left a parting word with the lady: "If you change your mind for any reason, please remember that I have already made you a proposal." With those words, he walked out of her life. It took several years and two broken relationships, both of which had nothing to do with him, for her gaze to turn in his direction. They are quite happily married today.

When you refuse to break into someone else's existing relationship, leaving the matter solely in God's hands, you are refusing to plow in someone else's backyard as it were. According to the law of sowing and reaping, such behavior will attract a harvest in time.

"Be not deceived; God is not mocked: for whatsoever a man soweth, that shall he also reap."

—Galatians 6:7

The individual is striving to ensure that he or she is walking worthy of the calling of the Lord, doing things that are blameless before men.

This is the way a Christian should maintain his/her integrity. The Bible puts it this way:

And if a man also strive for masteries, yet is he not crowned, except he strives lawfully
—2 Timothy 2:5

And every man that striveth for the mastery is temperate in all things. Now they do it to obtain a corruptible crown, but we an incorruptible.

—1 Corinthians 9:25

For this cause we also, since the day we heard it, do not cease to pray for you, and to desire that you might be filled with the knowledge of his will in all wisdom and spiritual understanding;

That you might walk worthy of the Lord unto all pleasing, being fruitful in every good work, and increasing in the knowledge of God;
—Colossians 1:9-10

SOME ISSUES RESOLVED IN COURTSHIP

Once courtship has begun between two consenting individuals, they would need to discuss a few issues to ease the relationship smoothly into marriage. But before we do this, it may be helpful to examine quite briefly, how the idea of non-conformism assists us in no small way to make the necessary adjustments.

NON-CONFORMISM AND THE CHRISTIAN

A born again Christian young man was on a transfer to a local community, where there was tremendous opposition to the Christian faith. Many friends of his interceded in prayer on his behalf that his faith in God would stand the test he was about to face. Since it was a temporary transfer, there was a great deal of excitement when he returned, and people were eager to hear the testimony of how he survived.

"How did it go, brother?" he was asked.
"Oh, very well, indeed," he replied.
"Did you have a lot of persecution?"
"Oh, not at all. I didn't let anyone know I was a Christian."

Several people feel this way when Christian principles clash with local cultural expectations. The feeling is: "Oh, don't stir the mud," they say, "it will only lead to more problems."

No one should stir the mud when issues that are not cardinal are in question. But cultural perceptions that entrench fears and distrust must give way to Christian principles that build love, intimacy, and a deep bond of friendship. "The way our people do it" may not be wrong in itself, except where it conflicts with Christian principles. Also, "the way our people do things" maybe perpetuating attitudes and perceptions that run contrary to one's new life in Christ. Abandoning such positions may lead to stresses and strains within one's cultural circles. Still, it is undoubtedly relevant to shine the light of the Gospel of Jesus Christ on practices and beliefs that do not engender wholesome godliness. We must never forget that it was due to such non-conformism that many of yesterday's twins are alive today, saved from infanticide by believing parents.

MONEY

In his letter to Timothy, the Apostle Paul, by the Holy Spirit, pointed out that the love of money is the root of all evil. (1 Timothy 6:10) It is clear from what the Bible has said that the problem with money is not the money itself, but the individual's attitude to it.

Our Lord Jesus Christ taught us a fundamental lesson about money and treasures and the related materials that portend to wealth.

Lay not up for yourselves treasures upon earth, where moth and rust doth corrupt, and where thieves break through and steal:

But lay up for yourselves treasures in heaven, where neither moth nor rust doth corrupt, and where thieves do not break through nor steal:

FOR WHERE YOUR TREASURE IS, THERE WILL YOUR HEART BE ALSO

—Matthew 6:19-21

The key to that lesson for individuals contemplating marriage lies in the verse that says: "For where your treasure is, there will your heart be also."

This Scripture is why most Christians would agree that as far as is possible, a couple should have their treasures together in such a way that their collective efforts sum up together and move in a single direction determined in the Lord. This approach to money is what we call having a JOINT FAMILY ACCOUNT.

A joint bank account is one of those teachings that help a couple develop trust in each other. In its simplest form, a joint bank account will be an arrangement where both the husband and the wife are signatories to the bank account, and either of their signatures is sufficient to withdraw money from that account. This arrangement is without any regard to the amount each contributes.

I agree with those who say that the husband should spend a certain amount of money without reference to his wife and that his wife should do the same. This arrangement creates a measure of freedom, particularly for those who initially feel somewhat suffocated by the process of integration. Such actions serve to ease-in integration rather than jump-starting it.

Experience has shown that a couple is better off, allowing the more discreet or, the more prudent party to do the transactions. I have seen and known families where the wife is the exchequer. For the husband to be the exchequer is more usual, but not exclusive, and both parties have independent access to the funds. It serves as a stabilizing influence in the early days when the bonds of integration develop in love and trust.

There are apparent pressures that militate against a concept like this, determined mainly by the prospective couple's cultural milieu. A young man was once told not to trust his wife since women are more open to spending temptations than men. As chauvinistic as this may sound, it was necessary to note that the advice is a usual saying in his cultural setting, and the adviser was not saying anything new.

Like we noted earlier, Christians should be constantly aware of these social and cultural pressures. One helpful thing is to remember that the Christian way of life is a culture by itself, determined by the principles and truth revealed in the Bible. It is relatively easy to lapse into our cultural milieu and say: "Oh, this is how our people do it." Indeed it may be, but the critical question should always be: "How does a Christian respond to a similar situation?"

I recall a story a brother told me years ago about his wife and his in-laws. At the very time in question, his wife's income was higher than his, and the concept of a joint family account looked like maintenance of the family by the wife. The lady's relations called her and advised her to be quite careful with her money, pointing out that "a woman does not feed a man." She related their "excellent advice" to her husband soon after the relations left.

During their next visit to the couple, it was her husband's turn to advise his in-laws. First of all, he thanked them very much for the advice they gave his wife. However, he pointed out that since both of them were now one, it would be better if they subsequently advised them together.

His in-laws were naturally embarrassed by the "leak," and felt their daughter was very foolish in "reporting" them to her husband. They never bothered to advise her on such matters after that.

I have seen this particular couple subsequently, and it is evident that the seeds of love and trust in their relationship, which they started to sow from the first day of their union, have paid off. They own a business of their own now and are quite reasonably comfortable, materially.

Some people have argued that couples who find it "impossible" to maintain a joint family bank account should run their finances separately to minimize areas of friction.

I suppose this goes without saying. But the couple must see themselves as being in an evolutionary process, where the central thrust of the change has to do with the transformation of the individual attitudes to material things. The more they can see money and like items as instruments to be used in fulfilling the purposes of God in their lives, the more they can pool their resources to fulfill God's purposes in their lives as a family unit.

The situation where one party sees the union as helping the other bear his or her family's responsibilities is, to say the very least, entirely unacceptable. It is intolerable because marriage makes the two people become one in every sense. The extended family responsibilities should never supersede the immediate family's needs. However, it is always good to remember that the two extended families' financial needs are inherited through the union. Any attempt at segregation will undoubtedly hurt the process of integration. The principle should be only to bite what you can chew.

There are situations where a man is sufficiently comfortable financially to feel he does not need his wife's "paltry" income. It is always good to bear in mind that having a joint family account is a principle that fosters integration. The amount of resources that each party brings to the fund is immaterial. What is essential is that the two parties are one as it concerns their finances, no matter how big or how meager.

I have recently become aware that prospective couples want to know how many brothers and sisters are in each other's family. This desire may sound rather strange since that information will become obvious much sooner than later. Said one young lady to me: "These days, they want to know how many you are in the family and your position in the family tree."

"Why do they want to know that?" I asked.

"Because they do not want to inherit family responsibilities by marriage."

It is not too difficult to see how attitudes change here in Nigeria, all in a matter of decades.

I recall the family life seminars that I attended years ago as a university undergraduate. The teaching was that "love and conviction should make you regard your wife's family responsibilities as your own, and vice versa."

I suppose that in societies where there are provisions for health and education, and some essential benefits for the unemployed, the aged, and the infirm, the question would not arise. Here in Nigeria, the extended family support system continues to prove the only significant safety net for society's vulnerable.

The challenge can be quite daunting in certain situations, but the words of Ruth to Naomi in Ruth chapter 1, verse 16, echo through the ages with great encouragement: "Your people shall be my people." Undoubtedly, a couple can only go as far as they can in these matters and no further. It is their responsibility to determine how far the Lord will have them go within the reality of their resources. Once the spirit of love and sacrifice rules us, then the Lord will enable us to do what we can, when we can.

However, some may say that it is entirely unnecessary, if not wrong, for a couple to put their relationship on the line because of their extended relations.

I suppose this goes without saying. The nuclear family unit, its stability, and welfare, and its very existence must take precedence over any other relationship. So it would be wise for a couple to try as much as possible to avoid any solo effort not agreed upon by the two parties. It is healthier to make every effort to achieve a consensus to enable the family to work together as a unit in every direction. A prayerful family will always discover that God has a way of getting us through life's challenges and situations.

Sometimes this realization comes to us in hindsight, which encourages us in the future to trust the Lord to enable us to do the things He has asked us to do for our extended relations and others around us.

CHILDREN AND FAMILY PLANNING

Some may feel that deciding on how many children to have and the interval between them during courtship is somewhat premature. The benefit of such a discussion is that one gains some insight into the other's thinking in an area that can create friction.

Some couples may decide that they would not have any children in the first year of their marriage. Such a decision often does not go down well with friends and relations. A close family friend told me why she and her husband had to abandon their decision to stay alone and enjoy each other's company for at least one year.

It is quite customary here in Nigeria for relations and friends to expect pregnancy to follow the wedding as soon as possible. This particular couple's friends had monitored them rather closely and had secretly prayed for them. Some of them had stopped by to tell them that they were praying for them to have children. They tried on several occasions to dispel the fears and anxieties of close relations with apparent nonchalance.

But by the sixth month after the wedding, it looked like what was a suppressed anxiety had become an open concern. The climax came when a group of Christian friends visited them, and one of them prayed thus: "Lord whatever the problem may be, solve it, and touch that womb in the name of Jesus," or words to that effect.

After they left, the couple felt that they had better assist the Lord more positively to answer this prayer.

Closely linked with the issue of children is that of family planning. A colleague of mine told me long ago of a vicar's wife, who was on her ninth pregnancy because the gentleman felt family planning was wrong.

A wrong attitude to family planning may pose severe health hazards for the woman, not only concerning the total number of children, but also the frequency with which they arrive.

In the Fellowship of Christian Doctors of Nigeria (FCDN), I have led several discussions on the family planning options available to the searching Christian couple.

I recall a young man in the medical school who attended one of these meetings some years ago and stated that "artificial" family planning methods were fundamentally wrong. His position was that family planning should only be done through faith and abstinence.

I asked him if he was married, and he said, "No." I then advised him to come back after he was married for a further discussion on the subject.

I recall some of us felt the same way years ago when we were single. The debate that day was quite heated at the FCDN meeting. A senior colleague then told us a comic story that quieted down the meeting hall. Said he: "There was this couple who believed that family planning was wrong, and that self-discipline, abstinence and safe periods were the only options available to the Christian. The couple decided to separate their bedrooms to reduce their periods of physical contact. They then decided to say their goodnight to each other in the living room and retire separately to their rooms when it was not safe to meet together because of the possibility of conception. This arrangement went on well for a good while. But soon, they realized that the crisp goodnight of yesterdays was no longer as crisp and that they lingered at the entrance to their separate rooms sorely tempted, but quite resolute. However, it soon became customary for the good night to be said in either of the rooms, and the obstetrician was soon to confirm to them how safe their method truly was when the pregnancy test proved positive."

I have always felt that once you accept family planning in principle, the question of what option to choose becomes a different matter. I have often said to those who advocate abstinence and safe periods as the only acceptable forms of family planning to note that they also accept family planning in principle. Their grouse is simply with the method.

A couple may express their reservations during courtship to reduce possible areas of friction. The situation whereby a woman has three children in three years can prove quite stressful if not debilitating. Raising children has physical, psychological, financial, and logistical implications.

When bunched together, three dependent children coming year on year can prove very stressful in today's world.

There are many family planning options available today, and a couple can always study what each option entails to assist them in making a choice acceptable to them.

A born again Christian is naturally opposed to abortion as a means of family planning. As a result, Christians have generally chosen family planning options that prevent conception, rather than avoid or tamper with implantation.

THE QUESTION OF SUBMISSION

Courtship is when an intending couple can begin to practice submission to one another as taught in the Book of Ephesians, chapter 5, verse 21:

Submitting yourselves one to another in the fear of God.

There is no doubt that any successful couple in this area would reduce their frictions within marriage to the barest minimum. Since this concept bears more directly on the married life, it would be more appropriate to defer it till then.

Courtship serves to reveal the degree of work that needs to be done in this area, which is cardinal to marriage stability.

DISCOVERIES OF COURTSHIP

How much of your past life should you tell a prospective spouse? Some say you should tell all where you went, who you went with, and what you did and pray that your partner would accept you despite all that. Others say that such detailed confessions are unnecessary since you risk breaking up the engagement in the process. They argue that such disclosures should be reserved when the relationship has sufficiently matured to accommodate such revelations.

A young man who never had "met a woman" was told all by his prospective wife. He felt somewhat disappointed by it and thought that it was as if he had kept himself pure in vain. A young lady who had kept herself pure thought it would be most unfair to be paired with a young man who had been "all over the town," as it were. It was like a shattered dream. She had prayed and believed that the good Lord would bless her with someone like her, who would just be chaste.

The Bible unequivocally declares in 2 Corinthians, chapter 5, verse 17:

Therefore if any man (any woman too) be in Christ, he

is a new creature: old things are passed away; behold, all things are become new.

We must add to this the Holy Spirit's injunction to Peter

in the Book of Acts chapter 10, verse 15:

And the voice spake unto him again the second time, WHAT GOD HATH CLEANSED, THAT CALL NOT THOU COMMON.

A new creature in Christ is new or cleansed before the Lord. Old things, including old records of sin, are passed away, and a brand new life in Christ has begun.

I suppose it is easier to accept your brother or sister despite their past if we are humble enough to admit that: "but for God's grace, there goes I or you." A situation where one is proud of his or her record of morality and virtue to the point of despising others will amount to sin before the Lord. The apostle Paul was careful to note in 1st Corinthians chapter 15, verse 10: "By the grace of God, I am what I am...'" Besides, what is implied by such attitudes is that certain sins are worse than others. Indeed from the human perspective, that may be so, but when the Bible equates brotherly hatred to murder (1 John 3:15), we may begin to gain some insight into how the Lord views sin. No wonder the Bible says in the Book of Romans, chapter 3, verses 9 to 12:

What then? Are we better than they? No, in no wise: for we have before proved both Jews and Gentiles, that they are all under sin;

As it is written, There is none righteous, no, not one:

There is none that understandeth, there is none that seeketh after God.

They are all gone out of the way, they are together become unprofitable; NONE DOETH GOOD, NO, NOT ONE.

THIS NOTE OF CAUTION

It is honorable to come clean with our significant past, so we do not practice deceit. The Holy Spirit will always guide the individual to the best timing to ensure it does not jeopardize the relationship. This transparency is particularly important in these days of growing HIV prevalence. Most Churches now require intending couples to do HIV tests in designated hospitals before they conduct the wedding. I recall an intending couple that brought an HIV negative test. But the marriage counselor insisted that the blood test be done at the designated hospital. It turned out that one of them tested positive for HIV. The other was shocked.

Certain sins leave their mark behind. HIV infection appears to dog the path of promiscuous people. We also see this in a few people who were transfused with blood infected with HIV.

Honesty and integrity demand that a young man or woman who had been "all over town" before being converted to Christ, should voluntarily undergo an HIV screening test before making or accepting a proposal. As a medical doctor in active practice, I am amazed at the percentage of donor blood or potential donors that screen positive for either HIV

I or II or both. A number of these carriers of the virus are young and single.

A youth counselor in a particular Church had cause to warn the young people, particularly newcomers, that the Church might begin to insist on HIV screening before approving a wedding involving any of their young men and women. Said he, "We would hate to see any of you come here and infect any of our boys or girls with AIDS." HIV screening test supervised by the Church has become mandatory for intending couples in practically every Church here in Nigeria. Quite a few carriers have been spotted as a result. The role of the Church in this regard is seen as an extension of public health.

I suppose this problem might prove quite a challenge in the future. One may foresee a situation where parents may demand mandatory screening before consenting to a marriage proposal. But a courting pair certainly would need to allay each other's fears in this regard, mainly if either or both of them had been promiscuous before conversion. Under such circumstances, an HIV screening test would help to allay any fears that may have arisen in both or either heart. That would be the honest way to address such a sensitive issue without spiritualizing it unduly.

OTHER REASONS TO TELL

I was told this story about a lady who had her womb removed by surgery but failed to communicate this information to her prospective husband. When the gentleman learned of this after the wedding, he naturally felt betrayed and concluded that the relationship was based on falsehood and must not be allowed to stand.

Some will say that one can always adopt children. Indeed, one can always adopt children, but not having the capacity to have one of your own should have been revealed, because the information was available before the marriage. Out of love and conviction, the individual may decide to adopt, or better still, believe God together for a miracle. The faith the other spouse may need to believe God for a miracle is likely to be affected by the bitterness from what they see as some form of betrayal of trust or deceit. Today, there are more options for couples to consider. These options include surrogacy which some couples have tried successfully by mutual consent. I refrain from making any comments about the morality of the procedure. I see it as compassion, but each couple must make their own decision prayerfully.

Some may argue that it is only under such clear cut situations that such information is available before marriage. In other circumstances, the individual may not be aware that such problems exist. If an individual is not aware that such a problem exists, they would have been walking in their integrity before God and man. It is easier under such circumstances to trust the Lord together. Let the power of agreement in prayer spoken about in Matthew, chapter 18, propel the couple to victory in the case in question.

I do not pretend to know the answer if one were to make a serious discovery of some vital information before the Church wedding. Suppose the aggrieved party decides to withdraw from such a relationship? In that case, there is no question that it will be divorce, particularly if they were married traditionally, and the marriage consummated albeit before the Church blessing.

Does the fact that there was a betrayal not justify a divorce? Should one be expected to forgive such a thing as deliberate deceit, and take on circumstances that he or she could have jolly well avoided, by excusing himself or herself with the plea of lack of faith needed to tackle the obstacle or problem?

I must confess that there are times I wish there were an epistle or epistles directed at these questions to make our walk easier for both counselors and counselees. Fortunately for the Corinthian Church, whose many unwholesome practices gave rise to the letters that give us a great deal of the insights that we have today, and unfortunately for us, they did not venture into these areas.

But be that as it may, there are principles in the word of God to help us. Any individual faced with this kind of dilemma should seek the face of the LORD ardently, and ask for grace from the ALMIGHTY GOD, to do whatever the LORD has laid on their heart.

INTIMACY DURING COURTSHIP.... HOW CLOSE CAN ONE GET?

In a sense, this question is inescapable in a book like this, particularly because there would appear to be real misconceptions about what should constitute the Christian approach to intimacy during courtship. Some time ago, a young man got up in a meeting to ask me what I thought 1 Corinthians, chapter 7, verse 36 meant:

"But if any man think that he behaveth himself uncomely towards his virgin, if she pass the flower of her age, and need so require, let him do what he will, he sinneth not: let them marry."

It might be helpful if we took the time to look at more modem translations. I think the way this verse is rendered in the C. E, Version helps a great deal:

But suppose you are engaged to someone old enough to be married, and you want her so much that all you can think about is getting married. Then go ahead and marry. There is nothing wrong with that. 1 Corinthians 7:36 (CEV)

I recall the way I answered the question on that occasion. "What is very important about that verse is not so much what it means, as what it does not mean. If you cannot tell what it means, concentrate on what it does not mean, which is more useful. It does not mean you can go to bed with a girl you are engaged to marry before you are married."

This approach is crucial for members of God's family called to shine as lights in a dark world. The Christian must have standards, below which he or she should not descend. 1 Corinthians, chapter 7, verse 37, speaks of self-control, which in itself is a fruit of the Holy Spirit (Galatians 5:23).

Having said they should avoid fornication before they are married, one may wonder how close intending couples can get. The answer is "not that close," and this is to prevent fornication. The danger of fornication is real, and this has floored those who trust in their strength and discipline. Arousing emotions you cannot satisfy would amount to some form of self-inflicted torture, which has often led some young people to the sin of masturbation and the like (1 Corinthians 6:9). This danger of immorality informs the position that it is best to keep away and wait for the fullness of time.

There are undoubtedly cultural variations on this question. There are communities where a warm embrace is a normal and acceptable form of greeting. In some cultures, it is customary to greet your guests with a light peck on the cheek. I suppose the apostle had this form of greeting in mind when he urged the saints to greet one another with a holy kiss (2 Corinthians 13:12, Romans 16:16, and 1 Corinthians 16:20). Those who contend that the apostle intended a distinctly holy kiss would advise those who sense that their kiss would not be that saintly to maintain a safe distance despite such a clear injunction. It would be fruitless to insist that one's kiss is undoubtedly holy, when torrents of emotions bubbling inside, speak eloquently to the contrary.

How far then can a courting couple go? The Holy Spirit is right there by your side to guide you on this very crucial question. The safest rule must remain never to go beyond your depth. Always keep safely away from the marriage bed until the priest has had the opportunity before the people of God, of pronouncing you man and wife, for that is where marriage must begin for the Christian.

The sensible thing to do for those who bum fiercely during courtship is to marry as quickly as possible. It is better to have a "low society" wedding with chastity than wait for a "high society" wedding and risk the loss of self-control and fornication. "It is better to marry than to burn."

7

WITH THIS RING I THEE WED

Once the two parties have pledged to live together for better for worse, then the review of all their years of Christian tutelage will commence. It will be time to show that they understand what the Christian faith is all about. It will be time to put Christian living principles that they both had learned to work in their union.

JACOB, LEAH, AND RACHAEL

Marriage creates the forum for proving the love between the two parties: That love can be so tangible as that of Jacob for Rachael, that it would indeed have the capacity to cover many sins. Rachael was a beautiful woman, and Jacob fell in love with her and was ready to pay any price for her.

Leah was tender eyed; but Rachael was beautiful and well-favored.

And Jacob loved Rachael; and said, I will serve thee seven years for Rachael, thy younger daughter.

And Jacob served seven years for Rachael, and they seemed unto him, but a few days, for love he had to her.
—Genesis 29:17-18 and 20 (KJV))

His prospective father-in-law Laban decided to exploit Jacob's love for his benefit. He first offered Jacob the tender eyed Leah, and when Jacob discovered the switch, he offered to serve another seven years for Rachael.

And it came to pass, that in the morning, behold, it was Leah: and he said to Laban, What is this thou hast done unto me? Did not I serve with thee for Rachael? Wherefore then hast thou beguiled me?

And Laban said, It must not be so done in our country, to give the younger before the firstborn.

Fulfill her week, and we will give thee this also for the service which thou shall serve with me yet seven other years.

And Jacob did so, and fulfilled her week: and he gave him Rachael his daughter to wife also.
—Genesis 29:25-28

But despite this apparent deep love that Jacob had for Rachael, circumstances in their lives put sufficient pressure on their relationship to evoke very angry responses.

And when Rachael saw that she bare Jacob no children, Rachael envied her sister; and said unto Jacob, Give me children, or else I die.

And Jacob's anger was kindled against Rachael: and he said. Am I in God's stead, who hath withheld from thee the fruit of the womb?
—Genesis 30:1-2

One would have thought that Jacob would never be angry with Rachael for any reason. But the pressures of life coming from many directions do get to strain human relationships. Our faith in God, the principles of Christian living that we have learned from the Bible, and the love for one another sustained in us by the Holy Ghost will help us be unchanging in our devotion to each other within marriage.

Therefore, this means that a good marriage is not necessarily one without disagreements or stresses and strains, but one within which the two people derive tremendous love and strength from each other, despite their circumstances.

I recall with gratitude to the Lord that I found myself unemployed one month after my wedding. What was quite significant about this experience was that my employer made me understand that my marriage appeared destabilizing.

But on looking back now, I could see the hand of Almighty God through it all. As a result of that experience, I veered to postgraduate work from private practice, where I ended up training as a physician and a nephrologist. And as a nephrologist, I have had the privilege of caring for quite a few people in my thirty-four years as a specialist physician. But there is no doubt that the experience did put our very young marriage under pressure.

After the euphoria and the wedding excitement have passed, it would be time for the real meat. The goal is to go through the initial phase of integration with minimal friction.

One thing that helps is to realize that Christians are not perfect people, and successful marriages are not about perfect people. Success is more likely to come to those who discover that what the Lord did was bring together two people who are perfect for each other. Therefore, success belongs to couples who strive after perfection daily and who invariably make mistakes in the process. As long as we keep our eyes on Jesus, we would continue to draw inspiration and strength to be what the Lord expects us to be in the world and the world around us.

THE LOVE WITHIN MARRIAGE

For purposes of rapid adjustment, a specific frame of mind is very useful. My wife or husband must be someone for whom I am willing to make a lot of sacrifices. To say, "Darling, I love you," to a spouse is quite reassuring, but to act in love consistently is even more so.

I have listened to many preachers, and teachers attempt to define and articulate Christian love, particularly as it relates to marriage. I have gained from all those studies and teachings that those who show love as consistently as they possibly could, are those who stop to think about it and progressively build it into their system. I have noted that passion is much needed to fuel self-sacrificing love. Once the sparks begin to dim and flicker, those who have not learned to love and care lose control of their relationship, and find themselves incapable of stoking the flickering embers to another radiant glow.

In this regard, studying a passage like 1 Corinthians 13 and appreciating the responsibilities of love becomes very useful. Such a quote helps us define what love is and what it is not. It bears repeating.

Love suffers long and is kind;
Love does not envy
Love does not parade itself, and is not puffed up;
Does not behave rudely

Does not seek its own
Is not provoked
Thinks no evil
Does not rejoice in iniquity
Rejoices in truth
Bears all things, believes all things, hopes all things, endures all things.
Love never fails
—I Corinthians 13:4-8

An individual can always ask himself: "Is this the kind of love I have for my spouse?"

A person may say: "I love my wife/husband very much." Indeed, you may, and you may be as sincere about it as your affirmation conveys. You should have no reason to doubt yourself. But if he or she were to add: "I have also learned to love my spouse very much," it would indeed be more reassuring. This approach reveals that they love their spouse when convenient, but they have also learned to love their spouse when it is not easy. They have developed an all-weather kind of love that can stand the test of time.

For a young couple tying the nuptial knots, talking about love in these terms may sound rather odd. But it is quite wise to realize very early in marriage that for love to be consistent, it must be very thoughtful. The mind and the spirit must always lean on the emotions to redirect them when they go negative. For example, a person justifiably hurt in a relationship may tend to react to that hurt. But the Spirit of God would instruct them through their human spirit to respond differently. The ability to respond the way we should each time is what makes us consistent in love. It offers our spouse something on which they can depend. Reacting the way we should each time is something we learn through a careful meditation on God's word and fellowship with other believers.

I have heard people describe a particular couple and say: "I wish I had a marriage like theirs."

The truth is that you could have a marriage like theirs, and even a better one, once you are willing to learn what it takes to produce one, and prayerfully believe the Lord. To think that it is a product of prayer alone is to commit the sort of error that the Bible spoke about in James chapter 2, verse 17, where it says: "Even so faith if it hath not works. is dead, being alone. "

I recall a sermon by Rev. Geoffrey Gardener in Ibadan in the seventies on love. He took quite an unusual perspective that day, using the experience of Joseph with his brethren. One thing that stuck with me from that sermon is the concept of forgiveness made available to the people, but which is withheld even at very great pains until the prospective recipients come to a place of repentance. Joseph had forgiven his brethren long before they appeared before him. He had seen God's mighty, unseen hands in it all when he became the Prime Minister of Egypt, next only to Pharaoh. But Joseph waited agonizingly for days and months for his brethren to come to a place of repentance before revealing his identity and offering them reconciliation. He considered one of the more painful responsibilities of love, where you withhold a deeply felt love in order to help the recipient become repentant and develop a godly and better character.

This perspective of love comes in very handy when one faces the upbringing of children, and a man and his wife must recognize it and appreciate it to use it for the benefit of their young family. Some will probably say: "Oh, don't you worry; we would rather cross that bridge when we get there." The danger in such an attitude is that things or rather events often overtake them, leaving them to do repair work, which is usually more painful.

UNDERSTANDING YOUR SPOUSE

Each party must make every attempt in marriage to understand the strengths and weaknesses of their spouse. One thing to bear in mind is that you did not marry to change your partner into what you want him or her to be. You married them to love and to hold, not as you would wish them to be, but exactly as they are with all their faults and shortcomings known and unknown till death do you part.

When someone marries their wife or husband, hoping that they would change, they are forever waiting for the person they married to emerge before giving their very best to the relationship. They are ever working to cause the partner of their dreams to appear. This kind of work is more often than not harmful because it consists of lectures, corrections, advice, and several reflections of a "better than thou" attitude, which is counterproductive.

One lady talked so much and worked so hard on her husband that he nicknamed her "Headmistress."

One should never marry with a hope to change one's husband or wife. If you cannot marry him/her the way he/she is, then do not marry them. That is not to say that people do not change in marriage; they certainly do. But when you marry to change your spouse into what you expect him/her to be, you create a dynamic that results in frustration.

The reason is not too hard to find. The individuals' attitudes to life were formed over the years in circumstances and environments tolerant or accommodating of him and his ways. They acquired the status of being right as far as they are concerned. For the wife or husband to come and expect all that to change overnight is a recipe for a great deal of misery and will often cause the marriage to take off on the wrong footing.

But when we accept our spouses as they are, we are in a position to assist them in becoming what we desire them to be in our home, not by lecturing them but by being worthy examples. I believe it is time to stop and look at God's word and what it teaches us about Christian homes.

MUTUAL SUBMISSION

Submitting yourselves one to another in the fear of God.

Wives, submit yourselves unto your own husbands, as unto the Lord.

For the husband is the head of the wife, even as Christ is the head of the Church: and He is the savior of the body.

Therefore as the Church is subject unto Christ, so let the

wives be to their own husbands in everything.
—Ephesians 5:21—24

Sometimes one feels that the issue of submission has either been skewed or deliberately over-flogged. I suppose the only reason some people think that way is that they believe that submission is only one-sided; that wives are supposed to submit themselves to their husbands in everything.

What we see is different. The first instruction is about mutual submission. This submission is qualified by the rider, "out of reverence for Christ." What this means is that marriage must impose certain constraints on both parties. They owe each other a standard duty of loyalty and dedication. The law of sowing and reaping (Galatians 6:7) will dictate that those who submit mutually to their marital union's demands reap the fruit of happiness, love, and stability. But those who feel that submission flows in only one direction create a master-servant scenario that many women find objectionable.

We will, however, need to study this concept carefully to appreciate why the Bible recommends it as the solution to relationship problems in marriage for believers in our Lord Jesus Christ.

A great deal has been written and said that the woman came from or out of the rib taken from Adam's side (Genesis 2:21-22). The implication supposedly is that God intended that a woman should be by the side of man, as a help to him, not above him, but not below him either.

I believe what the Bible has done with the concept of submission is to establish a chain of command in the home for responsibility and accountability. This order was put in place by God in the Garden of Eden because neither Adam nor his wife Eve was willing to take responsibility for what happened to them. In the beginning, Adam was not made the head of his wife by Almighty God. After they ate the fruit, and neither of them was willing to take responsibility for what happened, the LORD God made Adam the head of his wife to create a chain of command for responsibility with accountability.

But I would have you know, that the head of every man is Christ; and the head of the woman is the man; and the head of Christ is God.

—1 Corinthians 11:3

The family's chain of command is as follows: Christ is responsible to God for the Church, which is His body. The man is accountable to Christ for his family. He is to present his family to Christ and answer to Him concerning how he cared for them and led them in the ways of godliness and fellowship with Christ and His body, the Church.

The Bible says that the Lord will hold the husband responsible for what happens to his wife and children.

If men understood the depth and the demands of their responsibility, I believe there will be less talk about women's submission problems. The more significant challenge will be about what the men can do to ensure that they would have a great family they had nurtured to present before Christ when they appear before the Lord. A woman will be inspired to submit to her husband if she realizes that he is striving to do God's will on earth as it is in heaven. This focus on getting it right before God releases much grace and power to the family as they work and pray together.

SUBMISSION AND LEADERSHIP IN THE HOME

A young man about to tie the nuptial knot needs to know this about home management; submission is neither demanded nor forced; it is inspired in others by our Christ-like leadership of love and service to others. The best way to appreciate this is to look at our relationship with our Lord Jesus Christ. Our loyalty and commitment to Him is our simple way of showing appreciation for the great things He did for us in His life, death, and resurrection. The Bible summarizes it all beautifully in these passages:

Wherefore God also hath highly exalted Him and given Him a name which is above every name:

That at the name of Jesus every knee should bow, of things in heaven, and things in earth, and things under the earth;

And that every tongue should confess that Jesus Christ is Lord, to the glory of God the Father
—Philippians2:9-11 (KJV)

Neither is there salvation in any other: for there is none other name under heaven given among men, whereby we must be saved
—Acts4:.12 (KJV)

For scarcely for a righteous man will one die: yet peradventure for a good man, some would even dare to die.

But God commendeth His love toward us, in that, while we were yet sinners, Christ died for us.
—Romans 5:7-8 (KJV)

When our hearts are warmed by the joys of sins forgiven, when we sense an unusual boldness in us in confrontation with the powers of darkness, we bow in gratitude to our Lord Jesus for the struggle and the victory at Calvary's Cross. These are the things that enrich our sense of duty and loyalty to Him.

When a man loves and cares for all his family, they will follow him wherever he leads them, under God. They will find submitting to his leadership a joy because of the depth and quality of his love.

The other question relates to the concept of Christian leadership. I suppose a young man will only need to understudy our Lord Jesus Christ, to appreciate what the Lord expects of him as the head of his home. The Gospel of John, chapter 13, verses 12 to 17, is an excellent example.

So after He had washed their feet, and had taken His garments, and was set down again, He said unto them, know ye what I have done to you?

Ye call Me Master and Lord: and ye say well; for so I am.

If I then, your Lord and Master, have washed your feet; ye also ought to wash one another's feet.

For I have given you an example, that ye should do as I have done to you.

Verily, verily, I say unto you. The servant is not greater than his Lord; neither he that is sent greater than he that sent him.

If ye know these things, happy are ye if ye do them.

Our Lord Jesus Christ emphasized that whoever is the leader can only gain credibility for his position by being the example to follow. Once you can consistently lead the way through the correct examples, those who follow you would have no difficulty doing so. Some years ago, I recall, it was my privilege to counsel an intending couple the night before their wedding. I noticed that the gentleman was quite surprised when I emphasized that he must work at home as the head of the house, and no kind of job should be mean for him to do. I told him to remember to help with the scrubbing and the dishes and the cleaning. When I mentioned all these details, I noted that his eyes nearly came out of their sockets.

I heard the story of a Reverend gentleman in Nigeria with a Caucasian wife, who counseled his congregation to the effect that men should work at home, and show leadership in keeping the house tidy, looking after the children, doing domestic chores as much as they could. Most of the men in his congregation felt his problem was peculiar and thought he should not generalize what they considered his very personal experience.

I have come across men who have extraordinary ideas of what this leadership at home entails. This gentleman felt that his duty was to die for his wife if the need arose but not to do dishes or clean the house or help with the children. The wonder is that someone who does not love his wife enough to help with chores can suddenly rise to be her martyr. I would think that doing chores is infinitely less demanding than martyrdom.

The kind of leadership that our Lord Jesus Christ taught in the Bible is one that inspires followership naturally through consistent worthy examples of self-sacrificing love.

When John and his brother James expressed leadership ambitions through their mother, our Lord Jesus was very quick to caution them and steer personal aspirations in the things of God in the right direction.

But Jesus called them unto Him, and said, Ye, know that the princes of the Gentiles exercise dominion over them, and they that are great exercise authority upon them. But it shall not be so among you: but whosoever will be great among you, let him be your minister;

And whosoever will be chief among you, let him be your servant.

Even as the Son of man came not to be ministered unto, but to minister, and to give His life a ransom for many.

—Matthew 20:25-28 (KJV)

One way to appreciate working at home as an example of leadership for the man is to think of poor old Adam laboring under the weight of his domestic chores. The good Lord then looked on him in understanding pity and felt he needed someone to help him out. Those who believe that men should not work at home are implying that Adam hands off all his work when the woman arrived. Even if Adam did that, it would mean that he did not realize that what the good Lord sent was someone to help out only, not someone to take over all the chores.

Corresponding examples should always accompany leadership in the home. Parents who curse and swear, for instance, but expect their children not to do the same, may as well spare their breath, for as the saying goes: "The things you do, speak so loud that I cannot hear the things you say."

We may conclude this discussion on submission by saying that a man who desires submission from his family must be ready to lead them through examples of self-sacrificing love. That is the pattern left for us by our Lord and Saviour Jesus Christ the man's head.

LEADERSHIP FAILURES

A lot of the crises in most homes result from failure of leadership. In my years as a Christian and a member of Church groups and fellowships, I have studied leadership patterns. One thing that has come to me is that the most significant cause of leadership failure is when the supposed leader is not aware of what God expects of him as revealed in the Bible.

Leadership success is when the leader has learned to be led by the Holy Spirit of God through communion, instruction, and inspired obedience. Moses was a great leader in the Bible. His secret was that God led him through direct instruction. The Bible said that the LORD God Almighty spoke to Moses directly or face to face, the way a man speaks with his friend.

Our Lord Jesus Christ is the most astounding leader of all time. He told us His secret when He said in John 5:19: *The Son can do nothing of Himself except what He sees the Father do.* There is a good reason for this pattern. Our Lord taught us that God's will must be our command on earth as it is in heaven. Therefore, when men lead their families, they lead them by examples that model how to do God's will on earth as it is in heaven. Fathers on earth try their best to mirror our Father, who is in heaven. He could demand submission by decree; instead, He chose to command obedience through His love. He modeled His love in the sacrifice of His Son for our salvation.

Dear friends, let us continue to love one another, for love comes from God. Anyone who loves is a child of God and knows God.

But anyone who does not love does not know God, for God is love.

God showed how much He loved us by sending His one and only Son into the world so that we might have eternal life through Him.

This is real love—not that we loved God, but that He loved us and sent His Son as a sacrifice to take away our sins.

Dear friends, since God loved us that much, we surely ought to love each other.

No one has ever seen God. But if we love each other, God lives in us, and His love is brought to full expression in us.
-1 John 4:7-12 (NLT2)

Bible patterns and Bible principles are crucial to successful Christian leadership everywhere, particularly in the home, where we must be conscious that children often behave like photocopying machines. They tend to follow examples more than precepts. Parents who teach the truth of God's word but do not live a life of self-sacrificing love will find submission in their homes challenging to sustain.

For example, Mr. A may feel that this is the best way to solve a problem. His wife, Mrs. A, may share his view or may disagree. But if either or both of them can see what the Biblical principle or pattern is clearly or hear the Holy Spirit's communion pointing to the same thing, the path they should follow will soon become evident to them. This lifestyle of seeking direction from God in prayer and through the careful, balanced study of Biblical principles and patterns would sooner than later rub off on the children, who would then model their own lives accordingly.

The Bible teaches us to lead by example. When men lead their families without adhering to Biblical injunctions, young people quickly note hypocrisy and inconsistency. The Apostle James had this to say in James, chapter 1, Verse 22:

Be ye doers of the word, and not hearers only, deceiving your own selves.

When the husband and head of the home can take time in prayer and communion with his head, the Lord Jesus Christ, he will discover that his decisions end up blessing his family in multiple ways because of the wisdom of God distilled through communion and meditation. Besides the harmony and peace, there is the modeling of spiritual leadership in the home for all the family. He will also discover that the Holy Spirit is training him to practice self-sacrificing love in his family.

A Christian husband and his wife should discuss and share views on family issues. However, if there is a divergence of opinion or outright disagreement or differences, the man is to go to the LORD in prayer for wisdom and guidance to enable him to come out and say, "I can sense the LORD leading us this way." His wife must also be encouraged to do the same because they share the same Spirit of God in their lives. Even the children should be encouraged to go before the LORD in prayer. That is the way they learn how to make decisions as Christians. With time, the family will discover that God can guide through any household member and not just the father or mother.

When we hear from the Lord, we discover that the family's decision making process has become uncomplicated and straightforward. All we are doing is striving to know the mind of God, no matter who the spokesperson is. As head of his family, the man is the judge of who is the LORD's spokesperson. He discharges that duty with impartiality and integrity to model Christ to his family.

The problem will arise where the ego conflicts with the word of the Lord. Leadership failure will begin once a man or his wife sets their ego against the mind of the Lord. The simple way to avoid this kind of tragedy is to realize that we all are followers and that the Lord is the home's real leader.

This pattern also works both ways because we share the same Holy Spirit. When a woman follows the Lord, she would always go to the Lord to confirm a decision made by her husband. If she could sense that the Lord's approval is on the husband's decision, she should not hesitate to admit it to him. This attitude is the humility that breaks barriers for husband and wife. We do what the LORD is saying without bothering about who the spokesperson is.

I know a couple very well who wanted to buy a car. Mr.

B wanted them to buy car X, but Mrs. B. thought car Y was a more sensible thing to buy, given the limits of their known resources. Mr. B then asked Mrs. B only to say what she feels the Lord was saying to her. Mrs. B could not say it was her conviction from the Lord. She only felt car Y made more fiscal sense. Mr. B then urged Mrs. B to come along with his conviction and faith since she had none of her own. After weeks of dilly-dallying, Mrs. B finally agreed in prayer with her husband. It was a miracle and a testimony to the goodness of the Lord that within 72 hours after this prayer of agreement, Mr. B was able to mobilize the resources to buy car X, which has proved a great blessing to the family today.

Leadership success is a function of how effectively one can follow the Lord. Those who follow carefully and consistently lead well. Those who do not know how to follow the Lord cause the family ship to flounder in uncharted waters. Abraham showed how great it is to follow the LORD's instructions.

Now the LORD had said unto Abram, Get thee out of thy country, and from thy kindred, and from thy father's house, unto a land that I will shew thee:

And I will make of thee a great nation, and I will bless thee, and make thy name great, and thou shalt be a blessing:

And I will bless them that bless thee, and curse him that curseth thee: and in thee shall all families of the earth be blessed.

—Genesis 12:1-3 (KJV)

It may sound an exciting story, Abraham's move, but you will find that it was indeed a tall order for Abraham and all his family when you break it down to logistics. They were to be uprooted, every one of them, to an entirely new home. The head of the household got the instruction from the Lord. The rest of the family followed.

So Abram departed, as the Lord had spoken unto him; and Lot went with him: and Abram was seventy and five years old when he departed out of Haran.

And Abram took Sarai his wife, and Lot his brother's Son, and all their substance that they had gathered, and the souls that they had gotten in Haran; and they went forth to go into the land of Canaan; and into the land of Canaan, they came.

—Genesis 12:4-5 (KJV)

Sometimes, the burden of instruction from the LORD may be too heavy to share with the family. Most people believe that Abraham did not share this particular burden with Sarah, his wife. I think so also.

And it came to pass after these things, that God did tempt Abraham, and said unto him, Abraham: and he said, Behold, here I am.

And he said. Take now thy Son, thine only son Isaac, whom thou lovest, and get thee into the land of Moriah; and offer him there for a burnt offering upon one of the mountains which I will tell thee of

—Genesis 22:1-2 (KJV)

Abraham knew that this was one decision he could not share. The burden was too heavy to place on any other shoulder but his own. He shielded the rest of his family from the responsibility and bore it all alone by himself. This attitude is an excellent reflection of maturity in leadership. He had to sneak away from home in the early hours of the morning for a rendezvous with the Lord God Almighty.

And Abraham rose up early in the morning, and saddled his ass, and took two of his young men with him, and Isaac his Son, and clave the wood for the burnt offering, and rose up, and went unto the place of which God had told him.

—Genesis 22:5

Not even the two young men with him were allowed to distract him.

And Abraham took the wood of the burnt offering, and laid it upon Isaac his Son; and he took the fire in his hand, and a knife; and they went both of them together.

—Genesis 22:6

Isaac didn't get too many details either. Abraham bore the burden and the responsibility of that decision alone because he was sure it was from the Lord.

And Isaac spake unto Abraham, his father, and said, My father: and he said, Here am I my Son. And he said, Behold the fire and the wood: but where is the lamb for a burnt offering?

And Abraham said. My Son. God will provide himself a lamb for a burnt offering: so they went both of them together.

—Genesis 22:7-8

Undoubtedly, there are decisions like Abraham's decision in the life of a man and his family. Even the mere mention of it to a third party will dissipate the anointing and the resolve to follow the Lord. The consequences may not be as grievous as killing Isaac. But it often can be what will affect the family's economic and physical well-being if it fell through.

Decision making is part of the burden of leadership, and it is only men who have carefully learned to hear, obey and follow the Lord's instructions to the minutest detail that will bring an abundant blessing on their family. The Lord was pleased with Abraham and the resolve he showed in obeying the Lord as we read from Genesis 22, 15 to 18.

And the angel of the Lord called unto Abraham out of heaven the second time, And said. By myself have I sworn, saith the Lord, for because thou hast done this thing, and hast not withheld thy Son, thine only son:

That in blessing I will bless thee, and in multiplying I will multiply thy seed as the stars of the heaven, and as the sand which is upon the sea shore; and thy seed shall possess the gates of their enemies;

And in thy seed shall all the nations of the earth be blessed, BECAUSE THOU HAST OBEYED MY VOICE.

Abraham demonstrated excellent leadership ability for his home, which was nothing more than a manifestation of faithful followership of the Lord. Sarah, his wife, and the rest of his household showed a significant following of Abraham, which in effect was a tremendous indirect following of the Lord. The net result was immeasurable blessings from the Lord for all the family.

The most remarkable demonstrations of leadership failure in the home will be reflected by men who have not learned to follow the Lord and demonstrate resoluteness, firmness, and faith in doing so.

Once a woman and her children know that daddy will follow the Lord no matter what happens, their hearts would rest in following him, and accepting his leadership will come naturally. The Apostle Paul admonished the Church at Corinth in 1 Corinthians, chapter 11, verse 1:

"Be ye, followers of me, even as I also am of Christ."

A husband should be able to demonstrate this practically to his family as part of his leadership attributes.

THE FIVE STAR GENERAL

If we use a star to designate each responsibility, we may refer to today's wife as a Five Star General. The current worldwide pressure on low and middle-income family finances has compelled most young homes to be two-income families. In fact, in the world of today, this is the rule rather than the exception. If a wife is not working, the most likely reason is that she cannot find a job.

This Five Star General will have to be:
- A wife
- A Mother
- A HouseKeeper
- A Cook
- An Office worker/Businesswoman

The one thing that helps a woman fulfill these fivefold responsibilities in the home is to recognize them and apportion as much of her mental, psychological, and spiritual energy to each of them as the occasion demands.

Another thing that helps is a family that is very understanding, supportive, and appreciative. If the lady has a leader worth his name, who is not just grateful but is also leading by example, she will muster the inner strength and resolve to strive with joy, knowing it is a labour of love for her family. A man leading by example helps out where he can to make it a shared burden.

When we think of the young newly married lady as a mother, one may wonder whether it is not premature since the babies are still on the way. But failure to recognize that there are men who also look for a mother figure in their wives will lead to a good deal of unnecessary friction. A wife may also be looking for a father figure in her husband, someone to trust, someone to lean on for support at all times, someone with whom you do not doubt that you are always welcome, someone who is sensitive to your feelings and can detect your mood changes afar off. I believe it is vital to recognize these needs on time, allowing us to make the necessary adjustments.

Often, a fancy-free single girl recently married might find all these demands made on her just too much to contemplate. A young man gloating on the successful conclusion of a significant milestone in life may not be fully aware of the tremendous responsibilities thrust on his shoulders immediately.

Take the lady, for instance, before she got married, she was in the habit of flopping into a chair once she returned from her office. But now, she has a family to care for in five significant ways.

Those who recognize these roles and ask the Lord for grace and strength soon find that they can excel and surprise even themselves. In an atmosphere of love, they are bound to receive a lot of help from their husbands in the many ways they can contribute.

I recently heard of a man who was fond of complaining that the house was untidy each time he came from work. He concluded that his wife had been pretending in the earlier years of their marriage when she used to clean and scrub with vigor, or she was beginning to get lazy with time. One may wish to ask the gentleman what happened to his own hands, mainly because there was no one else to care for their four children and still earn an income into the bargain.

A "Five Star General" in the home may perform impressively, but it will be insensitive and unrealistic to believe that they cannot get tired with time.

THE FIVE STAR GENERAL AND INTIMACY

A young woman newly coming into wedlock may find the challenges of being the home's administrative manager quite daunting. Some find this so daunting that they give up, hoping that things will get done somehow, and somehow, they will get by. If they have a very understanding husband, he will prove an asset to their helpless state of mind.

Those who pursue their responsibilities with vigor find that they are so physically exhausted that all they wish to do is fling themselves into bed and sleep. Physical exhaustion contributes to emotional exhaustion.

A young man schooled in the Bible's writings may approach such a lady brandishing the precious words of I Corinthians 7:1-5, which says:
...It is good to live a celibate life.

But because there is so much sexual immorality, each man should have his own wife, and each woman should have her own husband.

—1 Corinthians 7: 1-2 (NLT)

The apostle says that rather than get yourselves messed up in fornication, go ahead, take a wife, accept a marriage proposal, and just get married.

The shock then is that even within the recommended solution of marriage, a man may still find that he is in danger of being messed up in fornication because his wife is always tired or has the "ubiquitous headache" each time he approaches her.

Someone has said that half of the headaches that women complain of each time their husbands approach them are not real but are convenient excuses. I have known ladies to admit that this is quite true and that it is a convenient way of saying that they are tired or turned off emotionally.

The apostle, however, went further to caution by the Holy Ghost:

The husband should not deprive his wife of sexual intimacy, which is her right as a married woman, nor should the wife deprive her husband.

The wife gives authority over her body to her husband, and the husband also gives authority over his body to his wife.

So do not deprive each other of sexual relations. The only exception to this rule would be the agreement of both husband and wife to refrain from sexual intimacy for a limited time, so they can give themselves more completely to prayer (and fasting). Afterward, they should come together again so that Satan won't be able to tempt them because of their lack of self-control.
—1 Corinthians 7:3-5 (NLT)

What is important to note is that this injunction is to protect the couple from immorality. I once read about an older preacher who advised the wife of a younger preacher with these words: "If you want your ministry to survive, you must keep your husband sexually satisfied, among other things." Each couple must face the responsibility if not the duty of satisfying each other's emotional needs. It is not an area in which one can afford to be whimsical or capricious. There is no doubt that those who have failed to note this injunction have paid dearly for it in the form of betrayed trusts, secret sins, or even broken marriages.

NOT A WEAPON OF OFFENCE OR DEFENCE

Sex within marriage is not a weapon of offense or defense. I know a young man who complained that his wife always used it against him. She would often say: "You will come and meet me in the night." She was known to "punish" him as it were for days or weeks. Another lady once said that she always advised her husband to concentrate more on praying since these matters are less important.

I have heard another lady quip that sexual needs are not like food, so the men shouldn't be complaining so much about denial.

All these constitute wrong attitudes to the sexual relationship within marriage, which Apostle Paul addressed by the Holy Ghost.

A young couple at the brink of their new life must determine to assist each other to avert sexual temptations. This attitude was what the apostle had in mind when he wrote in 1 Corinthians chapter 7, verses 8 and 9:

I say therefore, to the unmarried and widows. It is good for them if they abide even as I (i.e., if they can remain single).

But if they cannot contain, let them marry: for it is better to marry than to burn.

It will be ridiculous, to say the very least, to encounter people who are "burning" within a Christian marriage despite this very clear injunction to the saints. Besides, the danger to the individual's Christian testimony is quite real if he continues to burn persistently.

A young lady once thought that her husband was enduring her denials. She discovered quite tragically that he was letting off steam outside and was enduring nothing. Not too long ago, I learned about a gentleman who started to abuse himself within marriage through masturbation because of denial. The Bible is quite clear on the sexual responsibilities a couple owe to each other within marriage. It is in our best interest as Christian couples to carefully heed these bedroom teachings. These teachings help us keep the marriage boat sailing smoothly and the marriage bed undefiled by immorality.

THE FEELING OF BEING USED

I have heard several women complain that their husbands use them. They do not show any love, care, or concern until they have an urge. Then they come around and pretend to be romantic and cuddly. And as soon as you oblige them, they turn over and start to snore profoundly, indicating deep satisfaction.

This kind of scenario will create and deepen the feeling of being used in a woman. There will be the lingering feeling that she has deteriorated into a sex object for the amusement and pacification of her Lord and master.

I suppose this feeling will invariably occur when the man does not participate in the home except for his food and sexual satisfaction. The rest of the family life is left for the woman to sort out.

The Bible admonishes us to show love practically in 1 John 3:16-18:

This is how we have discovered love's reality: Jesus sacrificed his life for us. Because of this great love, we should be willing to lay down our lives for one another. If anyone sees a fellow believer in need and has the means to help him, yet shows no pity and closes his heart against him, how is it even possible that God's love lives in him?

This is how we have discovered love's reality: Jesus sacrificed his life for us. Because of this great love, we should be willing to lay down our lives for one another. If anyone sees a fellow believer in need and has the means to help him, yet shows no pity and closes his heart against him, how is it even possible that God's love lives in him?

Beloved children, our love can't be an abstract theory we only talk about, but a way of life demonstrated through our loving deeds. We know that the truth lives within us because we demonstrate love in action, which will reassure our hearts in his presence.

—1 John 3:16-18 (PassionNTPsa)

A couple should learn to show practical love to each other. Our Lord Jesus taught us that true love is always self-sacrificing. Through self-sacrifice, we know to do away with selfishness and pride and exchange them with humility and sacrificial living. The way forward is to help every couple, young or old, to follow our Lord Jesus' footsteps by loving, caring, and reaching out to each other. This approach is the way to live happily ever after.

If a woman complains of being used, then her husband must make every effort to correct that feeling by reaching out to her in other areas of their life. It is his responsibility to make her feel loved and wanted, not just physically, nor as a wife in the house, but as a very dear friend, whose company he has genuinely come to appreciate and cherish.

It is also his responsibility to ensure that his wife enjoys the act of sex so that she, too, can progressively become a willing and eager participant. Those who work hard in this area of their life to achieve harmony will reap a rich reward of stability sooner or later.

The error is to give up and sulk about the deficiencies that may exist initially. A young couple must realize that there are bound to be these deficiencies, mainly where they both arrived at marriage a little bit mystified about sex. There have been those for whom it was an anti-climax, leading to some degree of cynicism. For others, it has been a fulfillment of a long sought after liberation from chastity constraints. But no matter the perception at the onset, a deep-seated love for each other, sensitivity to each other's feelings, and communication that seeks to encourage rather than criticize will go a long way to promote happiness and joy in this area.

A WORD FOR THOSE WHO BURN

It might look excusable for those who "burn" within marriage to seek sexual satisfaction elsewhere, but it is nevertheless morally wrong. What should be the solution is to try and talk about it and openly admit your burning desires. Your spouse should be frank enough to put forward the things that put him or her off. After an open discussion like this, which should include an understanding of the Biblical principles outlined above, the two parties should resolve to ask the Holy Spirit of God to intervene in this area of their life together and break down the wall of differences.

This approach calls for patience and time of enduring while the Holy Spirit works out the grace within the two. It is good to remember that it is often at this time that the devil strikes with temptations.

A man in this situation should be careful about discussing his frustrations with an "available" lady. It may look like a signal to the lady to provide him with an emotional crutch to lean on, which may invariably lead to sin, breaking of the vow, and a breakdown of the marriage relationship.

A lady burning within marriage should avoid discussing her frustrations with an "available" man. The word "available" is used for sympathy or empathy from a vulnerable member of the opposite sex. This kind of exposure usually leads to sin.

Some years ago, I encountered a gentleman at a house fellowship meeting, which helped reveal this situation. I had just been led by the Holy Spirit to speak about the horrors of sin, particularly sexual immorality, how the Lord hates it, and how people involved should repent and come to Jesus. After the meeting, some of the guests gave their lives to Christ. This gentleman cornered me and wondered what he was doing wrong from what I said. He claimed that he had a lady friend who was "burning" within her marriage. He felt so "concerned" about her misery that he decided to "help" her out. Now "she is happy and feels quite satisfied. Her husband does not know, and my wife does not know either." Then he wondered, "What is wrong with that? If I leave her now, she will become miserable again.

Because of this warped or distorted reasoning, a couple must be careful about who and where they go to relate their problems. This gentleman's concept of help is nothing more than adultery, and wise old King Solomon has this to say on it:

Can a man take fire in his bosom, and his clothes not be burned? Can one go on coals, and his feet not be burned?

So he that goeth into his neighbor's wife; whosoever toucheth her shall not be innocent.

But whoso committeth adultery with a woman lacketh understanding: he that doeth it destroyeth his own soul.

A wound and dishonor shall he get, and his reproach shall not be wiped away.

For jealousy is the rage of a man, therefore he will not spare in the day of vengeance.

He will not regard any ransom; neither will he rest content, though thou givest many gifts.
—Proverbs 6:27-29,32-35 (KJV)

Rather than do that, the best thing is for the couple to seek their pastor or a spiritual marriage counselor to help them prayerfully adjust.

A couple with this problem should note that wounds inflicted here often run very deep, and the sooner they both bend and work at their relationship to improve things, the better their future.

Where there is a willingness to follow God's word and teachings, the solution is always in sight.

Our Lord Jesus Christ said in the Gospel of John, chapter 8 verses 31 and 32; *"If ye continue in my word, then are ye my disciples indeed; And ye shall know the truth, and the truth shall make you free."*

HANDLING UNFAITHFULNESS

One may come across a Christian couple who are battling with the problem of infidelity in their relationship. Proven adultery is a betrayal. It is a severe breach of trust as this Scripture reveals:

It is actually reported that sexual immorality exists among you, and of a kind that isn't found even among the Gentiles. A man is actually living with his father's wife!

—1 Corinthians 5:1 (ISV)

There are positive ways to approach the problem. Pray for the offending partner to genuinely repent and try as much as possible to love them while hating the sin they indulged in. It is essential to distinguish a one-off fall into sin from a chronic adulterer. A person overtaken in the sin of adultery should seek the face of the LORD for repentance and restitution. Nobody should treat an adulterer with kid gloves.

A lady once told me that the leaders of the men's fellowship in her Church told another lady whose husband fell into the sin of adultery that she should remember that men commit adultery with impunity in her culture. I thought that was scandalous. There is no place for indulgent sinning in the Body of Christ.

However, in sorting out the tragedy, we must establish that the fall was not due to burning within marriage, which is a spouse's denial of sex.

Also, there is a vital lesson to learn from Joseph, the husband of Mary. When he thought that Mary might have been unfaithful to him, he decided not to make a public fuss about it. But to quietly seek separation from the relationship. The Bible said that he decided to put his betrothed wife away quietly.

When as his mother Mary was espoused to Joseph, before they came together, she was found with child of the Holy Ghost.

Then Joseph her husband being a just man, and not willing to make her a public example, was minded to put her away privily.

—Matthew 1: 18-19 (KJV)

Joseph was going to put Mary away quietly without fanfare. Undue publicity about your spouse's sin may prove to be counterproductive. Approaching the pastor or the marriage counselor could prove helpful. But broadcasting it from the rooftop will humiliate the offending party and the entire family. Besides, you do not know who is listening or who will get to hear. They may be people who will make matters worse. It is essential to make every effort to regain rather than lose your spouse. (Matthew 18:15). In Psalm 32, verse 1, David said:" *Blessed is he whose transgression is forgiven, whose sin is covered.*"

An unfaithful person is required to repent and confess his or her fault to the offended spouse. The Holy Ghost's inspired wisdom should determine the timing of this confession and its desirability.

A young lady once told me that she would prefer not to know if her husband was overtaken in such a fault. She would prefer him to repent and change, away from such ways. The burden, she felt, would be too much for her to bear.

This attitude is why it is essential that the Holy Spirit takes control of each situation and decides what the offending party should do in each case and when.

An offending party who is not penitent risks the break up of his or her home. There is no room here for effrontery if one is truly born again. Pleading the usual besetting sin is self-indulgent and does not reflect a deep awareness of sin's gravity and how the Lord views it. Also, assuming that the individual's problem must be quite universal may be foolhardy since the issue before the individual is the problem that they have and not that of a hypothetical population.

The best approach for an offending party is to go before the Lord and confess that he or she really has a problem and so needs the Lord's grace and help to break away from the sin of adultery.

There are occasions where the individual needs to go into times of prolonged fasting and prayer to mortify the flesh through the Spirit as recorded in Romans chapter 8, verse 13." *For if ye live after the flesh, ye shall die; but if ye through the Spirit do mortify the deeds of the body, ye shall live."*

THE FAMILY ALTAR

A family altar is where the couple can meet to strengthen each other through meditation in the word of God and prayers. This session should not take the place of the individual's prayer walk with the Lord but should be a time for the family to share and grow together.

The pressure in today's world may harm this age-old tradition whose benefits for the family are tremendous. Every effort must be made by the couple to share a regular time of prayer and meditation. If they started praying together during the courtship period, it would be easier to ease into a routine after the wedding.

Those who have constraints concerning regularity must endeavor to have quality family prayer times, where faith is transmitted to the other family members by the man and his wife. This transmission is particularly important when the children begin to arrive on the scene.

There are daily Bible guides that are quite useful, and for those who are not too familiar with this, the usual pattern is to:

- Sing hymns and or choruses to praise the Lord

- Read the Bible passage for the day with each literate adult and child participating

- Expand the thoughts and revelations contained in the selected Bible passage and ask each member of the family to contribute a view where they can, with the father or mother moderating

- Ask each participating member for their prayer needs, and then go to the Lord in prayer, remembering these personal needs and the general needs of their friends and the society and nations.

This session usually takes about 20 to 30 minutes, and a family should find time for this daily.

8

LEADERSHIP IN THE FAMILY AND CHURCH/FELLOWSHIP RESPONSIBILITIES

The Bible declares that those who lead in the Church should be known to lead well in their homes. In Paul's letter to Timothy, he stated to the young Bishop that Church leaders must be examples of Christ in character before they qualify to lead the Church of God.

If a man desires the office of a bishop, he desireth a good work.

A bishop then must be blameless, the husband of one wife, vigilant, sober, of good behavior, given to hospitality, apt to teach;

Not given to wine, no striker, not greedy of filthy lucre, but patient, not a brawler, not covetous;

One that ruleth well his own house, having his children in subjection with all gravity;

(For if a man know not how to rule his own house,

how shall he take care of the Church of God?)

Not a novice, lest being lifted with pride he fall into the condemnation of the devil.

Moreover he must have a good report of them which are without; lest he fall into reproach and the snare of the devil

—1 Timothy 3:1-7

The ideas expressed here impose tremendous responsibilities on the head of the home. It is beneficial for us to examine each of them to appreciate better the duties inherent in the leadership of the home and how it inter-relates to leadership in the Church of God, be it a fellowship group or a denomination.

A BISHOP MUST BE BLAMELESS

This quality implies that a man who aspires to leadership in the family of God must do all in his power to reflect Christ's life to the world. In addressing the Church's questions at Thessalonica, the Apostle had this to say about this quality of being blameless.

Now we command you, brethren, in the name of our Lord Jesus Christ, that ye withdraw yourselves from EVERY BROTHER that walketh disorderly (i.e., in a blameworthy way), and not after the tradition which he received of us.

For yourselves know how ye ought to follow us: for we behaved not ourselves disorderly among you;
—2 Thessalonians 3:6 (KJV)

The Apostle himself spoke about his struggles to show that he walked in an orderly manner before the saints, combining precepts with practice.

Know ye not that they which run in a race run all, but one receiveth the prize? So run, that ye may obtain.

And every man that striveth for the mastery is temperate

in all things. Now they do it to obtain a corruptible crown, but we an incorruptible.

I therefore so run, not as uncertainly; so fight I, not as one that beateth the air:

But I keep under my body and bring it into subjection: lest that by any means when I have preached to others, I myself should be a castaway

—1 Corinthians 9:24-27 (KJV)

THE HUSBAND OF ONE WIFE

As a preamble to this discussion, it is essential to note that there are societies where bigamy or polygamy is against the law. In other words, having more than one wife at any given time, in such communities or nations, is against the law of the land. However, in traditional societies, particularly in Africa, Muslim and oriental communities, it would appear that either bigamy is accepted or condoned, or the law generally turns a blind eye. The woman at the well in John chapter 4 presents the classic picture of progressive bigamy. Said Jesus to her, "you have had five husbands, and are currently cohabiting" (John 4:16-18).

What the Apostle Paul had in mind here, when he wrote that a Bishop should be the husband of one wife, was the latter kind of society where having more than one wife was acceptable under the law.

There is considerable controversy in the Church of God today concerning this aspect of home life and how it should relate to leadership roles in the Church of God. A bishop or church leader should be the husband of one wife.

There is universal agreement amongst the Churches that any serious born again Christian who goes to take an additional wife is walking disorderly and should undergo disciplinary measures from the fellowship up to timed ex-communication that should subsist until he purges himself.

"...that ye withdraw yourselves from every brother that walketh disorderly,"

—2 Thessalonians 3:6

But now I have written unto you not to keep company,

if any man that is called a brother be a fornicator, or covetous, or an idolater, or a railer, or a drunkard, or an extortioner; with such an one no not to eat

—1 Corinthians 5:11 (KJV)

But what should happen to the man who was married to two wives before he was born again? This pre-conversion polygamy is the controversy amongst believers, particularly here in Nigeria. What should they do with their other wives?

There are two primary contending schools of thought that claim to represent the Bible position on the subject. The first one, is the more popular it would appear. In effect, it says that the man should quietly allow his other wife or wives to disengage but should be responsible for their upkeep and that of their children. From the moment he realizes this, he should cease to have conjugal relations with her or with them as the case may be, and restrict his affairs to his first wife.

Where the woman or women to remarry, he and his first wife should take up the responsibility of raising all the children. They should, as much as is humanly possible, show no kind of partiality between the children.

I have heard the second and third wives often grumble that all that the new birth experience has done is destabilize their homes and render their children practically fatherless. Some couples have accepted this position, disengaged from their wives amicably, and taken responsibility for their children and their wives until they all remarried.

Those in favor of the view expressed by the second and third wives, as the case may be, say that the Apostle was only concerned about leadership in Church. There is, therefore, no justification for rendering children fatherless and disorganizing existing families. Therefore, a man with two wives may serve the Lord in several capacities but not as a leader, since as a leader, he is to be the example for others to emulate.

The implication is that once a man has married two wives, he has married two wives. Sending them away will still not alter the fact that he has been married to more than one wife. Therefore, he does not qualify to assume an apical leadership role in the New Testament Church of Jesus Christ.

The reason why I have added New Testament Church is that some contend that the issue of the number of wives a man had did not appear to have mattered at all with the Old Testament men of God. In fact, in indicting David for his adultery with Bathsheba, the prophet implied in 2 Samuel, chapter 12, verse 8, that if wives were his problem, he should have approached the Lord directly.

In discussing with the Jews of His time, our Lord Jesus Christ explained that some of these Old Testament practices were allowed as expediencies but were not God's ideal mind. A case in point here was divorce.

They say unto Him. Why did Moses then command to

give a writing of divorcement, and to put her away?

He saith unto them, Moses because of the hardness of

your hearts suffered you to put away your wives: but

from the beginning, it was not so:

—Matthew 19:7-8

When the Apostle led by the Holy Ghost admonished that the bishop or deacon must be the husband of one wife, he excluded all those who had more than one wife from holding such an exalted office in the Church. There is nothing there to suggest that those who had more than one wife could send their wives away to qualify to be a bishop or a deacon. They do not qualify pure and simple. Nobody suggested that sending their wives away will alter their status.

There was a man who had a wife of ten years. She happened to be his second wife. He had separated from his first wife. He got converted and wanted to serve the Lord as a minister of the Gospel. His Church told him that the only way he could do that was to get rid of his two wives' status. He promptly asked his wife of ten years to move on. I thought it was outrageous.

The gentleman could serve the Lord in many other capacities, but not as a pastor or a deacon. He could witness to God's grace, preach and teach, serve with evangelistic teams, and try to reach others with the Gospel of Jesus Christ.

I can sense the Holy Spirit's mind in the injunction on monogamy being the norm for bishops and deacons. It maintains order and discipline in the Church and establishes the highest moral standards of conduct for the Church leaders and elders.

However, some argue that the issue of a man's position outside of grace, that is before he or she was born again, must qualify for what the Apostle Paul aptly described in Acts 17, verse 30 as "Times of Ignorance." They contend that if a man is willing to repent and make the necessary restitution (i.e., send away his "extra" wives), he may be allowed to lead the flock of God as an overseer or a pastor or a Bishop. This sort of ruling does not consider the fate of the women and children sent away.

To the second school of thought, it is essential to note that we are saved kings and priests unto the Lord. The spiritual position of a man saved while having more than one wife is not in doubt. It is his role within the Church that is in question. What the Apostle said by the Holy Spirit is that he should not be made a deacon or bishop to avoid confusing the Church. But he can minister with his gifts and calling to the glory of God.

If his wives are quite happy to stay with him, there is no reason to put them away as some teach. He is at liberty to continue to seek the Lord and grow spiritually. He should be available to the Lord to serve Him in any way the Lord Himself deems fit; witnessing, serving, preaching, and teaching at various levels, as the case may be. This approach does not, in any way, set aside the Holy Spirit's rulings designed to maintain order and discipline in the Church of God. But it saves women and children from being thrown into an uncertain future and life.

In summary, then, what we are saying here is what the Bible has stated clearly:

- A bishop or deacon should be the husband of one wife. This ruling sets the standard for every man and every woman in the Church of Jesus Christ.

- Men with more than one wife before they were born again may be presumed to have done so in ignorance. However, they may not hold office in Church as a bishop or a deacon or an elder.

- Getting rid of their second or more wives should still not qualify them to be a bishop or a deacon in the Church. That does not mean that they cannot have the calling of God to minister in an office where the anointing exists. But administratively, their position in the Church should always be subordinate to the overseer. It should not be apical. This arrangement is because the commandment was to set standards and so maintain organizational discipline.

- If a brother who is born again goes ahead to take more than one wife, he is walking disorderly and should be excommunicated. By his action, he refuses to accept the Bible as the final authority on all Christian conduct and behavior. If he repents, part of the restitution to be demanded by the Church for the sake of order and discipline is that he separate from this so-called new wife before he can rejoin the fellowship.

- Should a man with more than one wife before he was born again send away his wives as a form of restitution? I believe the man has no right to send out his wives or deny them their conjugal rights. To do that will create disorder and promote immorality in the family of God. I must admit that the decision lies with the individuals directly concerned. If children are involved, it becomes a little more complicated because of their physical, financial, and psychological health. Those who feel led to separate, who also have no offspring in the marriage, may do so and pray for the grace to be chaste until they remarry. Those who separate and choose not to remarry must pray for the grace to spend their days serving the LORD. But anyone withdrawing from such a relationship should only do so by conviction and volition, not as an ordinance. Those who initially chose not to remarry are at liberty to change their minds in the future, as the Biblical principle reveals.

Have you been bound to a wife? Stop trying to get free. Have you been freed from a wife? Stop looking for a wife.

But if you do get married, you have not sinned. And if a virgin gets married, she has not sinned. However, these people will experience distress, and I want to spare you that.

—1 Corinthians 7:27-28 (ISV)

I believe that this is the mind of the Lord on this matter. It is love in action to protect children born into this setting from untold miseries and agonies.

- It is important to note that what I have shared concerning events before grace is different from events within the dispensation of grace. The Apostle Paul was careful to mention to the Church at Corinth that the two situations are different.

For what have I to do to judge them also that are without?

Do not ye judge them that are within?

But them that are without God judgeth. Therefore put

away from among yourselves that wicked person

—1 Corinthians 5:12-13 (KJV)

Again, he noted earlier in the same chapter how important it is to maintain order and discipline within Christ's body.

Know ye not that a little leaven leaveneth the whole lump?

Purge out, therefore, the old leaven, that ye may be a new lump, as ye are unleavened. For even Christ, our Passover is sacrificed for us:

Therefore let us keep the feast, not with old leaven, neither with the leaven of malice and wickedness; but with the unleavened bread of sincerity and truth.

—1 Corinthians 5:6-8 (KJV)

I would imagine that for a good number of believers in the affected societies, questions will remain, mainly because of the ambivalence in many churches' practices. Let us say that the Church has a responsibility to streamline conduct in line with the mind of the Lord, to maintain discipline and moral standards of the highest level. This obligation is why the Church should excommunicate the brethren who are disorderly and disruptive in their behavior.

However, for those who still have questions on their mind, let us take solace in Apostle Paul's admonition to the Philippian Church.

Let us, therefore, as many as be perfect, be thus minded: and if in anything ye be otherwise minded. God will reveal this even unto you.

Nevertheless, whereto we have already attained, let us walk by the same rule, let us mind the same thing.

—Philippians 3:15-16

What I have stated here is what I believe is the Lord's mind on these issues, designed to set order in the Church of God.

We are all called to walk in conscience before the Lord. The Apostle Paul admonished that those who forsake their conscience make shipwreck of their faith (1 Timothy 1:19). Those who mistake grace for a license to sin get a rebuke in Romans chapter 6. No one can use God's word to walk disorderly and still claim to walk in conscience before the Lord.

VIGILANT, SOBER, OF GOOD BEHAVIOUR

This condition is akin to the Apostle Peter's call to the Church in 2 Peter 1:5-10, to the intent that we should add virtue to our faith in several areas of life. A young man leading his family with vigilance, soberness, reflecting good behavior, will soon find that the Lord is calling him to lead the family of God's people as well, in one capacity or the other.

GIVEN TO HOSPITALITY

A young couple must always bear these Holy Ghost inspired Pauline admonitions in mind.

Let brotherly love continue.

Be not forgetful to entertain strangers: for thereby some have entertained angels unawares

—Hebrews 13:1-2

And let us not be weary in well doing: for in due season we shall reap if we faint not.

As we have therefore opportunity, let us do good unto all men, especially unto them who are of the household of faith.

—Galatians 6:9-10

APT TO TEACH

This condition will represent the fruit of their study of God's word in obedience to the admonition that the Apostle Paul gave to his son in the Lord, Timothy.

Study to show thyself approved unto God, a workman that needeth not to be ashamed, rightly dividing the word of truth.

—2 Timothy 2:15 (KJV)

Their study should cover all of God's word because;

All scripture is given by inspiration of God, and is profitable for doctrine, for reproof, for correction, for instruction in righteousness:

That the man of God may be perfect, thoroughly furnished unto all good works

—2 Timothy 3:16-17 (KJV)

NOT GIVEN TO WINE

A young couple must recognize that if they are in the habit of drinking alcoholic beverages, the Lord will not trust them with much responsibility for the Kingdom.

I think the problem with alcohol is its capacity to undermine the individual's moral resolve and impair his judgment, as Solomon noted in Proverbs 31, verses 4 to 5.

It is not for kings, O Lemuel, it is not for kings to drink wine, nor for princes strong drink:

Lest they drink, and forget the law, and pervert the judgment of any of the afflicted.

HE MUST BE NO STRIKER

In other words, he should not be a boxing champion, particularly in his home. There is nothing that demeans a man more before his wife as when he stoops so low as to beat her physically. Those who do this may do so in a fit of anger or under the influence of alcohol. No wonder the Apostle also said that the fellowship or Church leader should not be a habitual alcoholic beverage drinker.

A young couple should bear in mind what the Bible says about the wrath of man.

Wherefore, my beloved brethren, let every man be swift to hear, slow to speak, slow to wrath: For the wrath of man worketh not the righteousness of God.

—James 1:19-20 (KJV)

He that is slow to wrath is of great understanding: but he that is hasty of spirit exalteth folly.

—Proverbs 14:29 (KJV)

There is no need to hide under the umbrella of the so-called righteous indignation. Our Lord Jesus demonstrated what is meant by righteous indignation when He whipped the money changers out of the temple in John Chapter two. They were converting the temple of God into a madhouse of merchandise.

The Apostle Paul admonished by the Holy Ghost:

Be ye angry, and sin not: let not the sun go down upon your wrath.
—Ephesians 4:26

A young couple may do well to heed these injunctions if they desire the Lord to use their lives to touch other lives for the Kingdom.

NOT GREEDY OF FILTHY LUCRE, NOT COVETOUS

We had discussed a couple's attitude to money when we were looking at courtship. Concerning leadership responsibilities, a couple must develop a high degree of fiscal discipline that will enable them to lead the Church of God entrusted to them, whether it be a home fellowship, or Bible Study Group, or a Church denomination.

The problem that has emerged in recent times has to do with young couples who are "pastor founders" but have not correctly organized their church or denominational finances.

If they are not self-funding, they should take a salary that should attract a review betimes to match the Church or group's growth and the local economy's reality.

In this age of computers, this aspect of Church life has been made a lot easier. A church can easily acquire a small personal computer and an accounting package that will help them organize their finances so that anybody interested may see the Church's financial growth records.

A situation whereby there is no distinction between the pastor's money and that of the Church is unacceptable, to say the very least, and may expose the young couple to possible charges of financial impropriety. A young couple running a fellowship or church group must reflect that they are not in it for the money and have nothing to hide.

Recent publicized experiences in the USA's Church family have shown that a lot of prudence and care is required in this area by young couples in leadership roles in the family of God. I do not doubt that this is the same for our Churches in Nigeria and other parts of the world.

ONE THAT RULETH WELL HIS OWN HOUSE

Of all the leadership requirements that confront a young man, this appears to be the most cardinal. It relates directly to his performance at home.

One that ruleth well his own house, having his children in subjection with all gravity;

For if a man knows not how to rule his own house, how shall he take care of God's Church?

—Timothy 3:4-5 (KJV)

Some years ago, a young lady evangelist told us a story of her experience in a particular Church. She had gone there on an invitation to minister to this congregation and was a guest at their worship leader's home. On one of the days, she went out and came back to meet the worship leader's wife in tears due to a quarrel with her husband. When she got to the Church, the worship leader was already ministering at the podium. She had to stop him. She told him to go home and reconcile with his wife before coming to rejoin them.

I believe that one of the help a young man receives in marriage is that he can serve the Lord better with fewer distractions, particularly those who, like me, do not possess the rare gift of celibacy. But then, he has the added responsibility of ensuring that marriage becomes the springboard for greater effectiveness which it should be, so that two can indeed put ten thousand to flight as opposed to one just putting one thousand to flight (Deuteronomy 32:30).

Therefore, a young man must learn to rule his household well under the Lord and raise his children in subjection and the fear of the Lord.

HIS PUBLIC IMAGE

He must not be a novice who will have problems with pride. He must be mature and maintain an exemplary public image among non-Christians. In other words, a young man must endeavor to reflect qualities that will not attract a sneer when people mention his name.

One has encountered this now and again when people who have not been born again come forward to say that they and a supposedly born-again Christian meet in all kinds of places they didn't think people like him should go.

I once heard the story of a young lady who felt going to discotheques was not necessarily un-Christian. While a gentleman engaged her on the dance floor, she decided it was an opportunity to witness.

'You will need to be born again, you know," she began. The gentleman was upset by the intrusion. He acidly reminded her that people who are born again do not come to that kind of place.

It is no secret that people outside the Christian family, and by that I mean the born again Christian family, know what a born again Christian should be doing, even when they do not subscribe to such standards themselves.

A young man's public image may be his affair, but if he wants the Lord to use him, then his public image and testimony must be of great concern to him. The Bible refers to believers as ambassadors of heaven, who must pass on God's message of reconciliation to the world lost in sin and bound by the devil.

CONCLUSION

The bearing of leadership qualities on marriage may seem out of place. People usually do not think of marriage in such terms. To some, marriage should merely be falling in love with someone and just whisking them away to the nearest priest to make the necessary vows. But if we remember that the calling of the Lord on our lives is one calling, then marriage and every other area of our lives are designed to help us to be what the Lord will have us be everywhere and every time. We must assist each other as husband or wife and as members of the body of Christ, "Till we all come in the unity of the faith, and of the knowledge of the Son of God, unto a perfect man, to the measure of the stature of the fullness of Christ." (Ephesians 4:13).

9

ONE IN AND ONE OUT

As mentioned earlier in this book, one of the most significant marriage travails comes when one party is born again while the other party is not. In a society like Nigeria, where the culture favors a dominant male community, it can be quite terrible for the woman to convert to Christ and live with a husband who is not. Most of these men usually try to use their authority as head of the home to obstruct the woman's practice of her faith, creating many dilemmas. This tense situation brings up Prophet Amos' rhetoric question in Amos chapter 3, verse 3:

"Can two walk together except they be agreed?"

But walk together, they must if both desire to spend eternity with our Lord Jesus Christ. The fact that one's husband or wife is not born again is not a basis for separation or divorce. The Bible in 1 Corinthians, chapter 7, verses 12-14, is quite clear on this.

I (not the Lord) say to the rest of you: If a brother has a wife who is an unbeliever and she is willing to live with him, he must not abandon her.

And if a woman has a husband who is an unbeliever and he is willing to live with her, she must not abandon him.

For the unbelieving husband has been sanctified because of his wife, and the unbelieving wife has been sanctified because of her husband. Otherwise, your children would be unclean, but now they are holy.

—1 Corinthians 7:12-14 (ISV)

Therefore, continuing to live together is a great challenge for the party that first saw the light of the Gospel of Jesus Christ. Being Christian in an unchristian home environment attracts some form of persecution invariably.

A brother once confided that he spent eight good years praying that the Lord would touch his wife. Later on in their life, events proved that the lady would still require a second touch since the first one was not deep enough to cause a permanent change in her life.

Those who have passed through this experience testify very eloquently that the two key things that work wonders in a spouse's conversion are practical Christianity and deep and intense intercessory prayers. Nothing else will work a miracle. Practical Christianity is another way of saying the manifestation of the Holy Spirit's ninefold Fruit at home - love, joy, peace, patience, goodness, kindness, faithfulness, meekness, and self-control. Unconditional love will work wonders. Goodness and kindness are tools of friendship. They serve to develop bonds of friendship between the two. Patience and self-control suffice to weather storms, so we never use words that hinder but say only things that help. Through faithfulness, we learn to hold steady under pressure, while meekness imparts a glow to all our labors of love. With joy, we maintain the right atmosphere for positive impact at all times.

THE DILEMMAS THAT EXIST

The most severe dilemma arises when the unbelieving spouse's desires directly conflict with God's word. A certain man was under pressure at work. He decided to consult some native doctor in his village who prepared a dead chicken potion to drive the evil forces away. The Christian lady found this intolerable because the dead chicken filled the whole house with a stench. Indeed a woman is called to submit to her husband, as unto the Lord. We must appreciate what this means and understand the context and the spirit behind it. Two key verses quoted earlier call for closer scrutiny.

Wives, submit yourselves unto your own husbands, as unto the Lord.

Therefore as the Church is subject to Christ, so let the wives be to their own husbands in everything.

—Ephesians5:22 & 24

The lady in the above story is not expected to welcome this dead chicken to solve the husband's workplace problem.

There was another lady in a particular Church who was born again, while her husband was not. She claimed that her husband had always insisted that she follow him to his Church in another city. After a lot of hassle at home, she decided to go just once and see what kind of service it was. What she found shocked her no end. The object of worship was a giant tree. The worshippers were required to be clad very lightly but quite indecently. The service itself involved a weird dance round and round the tree, chanting choruses like a bunch of drunks. She felt great pity for her dear husband and wondered what such an intelligent person was doing in a place like that. She never went again despite repeated pressure. It was evident that this was not part of what the apostle had in mind when he admonished the wives to submit to their husbands. It was like the apostle knew there would be situations like this, which was why he added, "as unto the Lord."

Several years ago, I met a young lady who faced a similar kind of dilemma. This time she was to participate in a ritual to appease the gods. Out of loyalty to her husband, she went ahead and performed the ceremony, only to discover that she had incurred the displeasure of the Lord.

Wives are to obey their husbands as unto the Lord.

This injunction implies that they should obey their husbands because of the Lord, or as one would do it to the Lord.

It should not be like the proverbial lady who learned about this Biblical injunction of obedience to her husband. Said the lady, "Whoever wrote that does not know my husband. If he did, he would never have written it. I know my husband, if you do that, he will ride you like a donkey." Verse 25 of Ephesians chapter 5, says the manner is similar to the way the Church is subject to Christ. The Church's subjection to Christ is voluntary, in response to the love and sacrifice of Christ. The Bible declares in the first general epistle of John chapter 3, verse 16:

Hereby perceive we the love of God, because he laid down his life for us: and we ought to lay down our life for the brethren.

—1 John 3:16

Herein is love, not that we loved God, but that he loved us, and sent his Son to be the propitiation for our sins

—1 John 4:10

A husband who participates in the worship of other gods or idols cannot expect his wife, a born again Christian, to follow him there. The Bible protects the born again Christian woman because the injunction says it is as the Church is subject to Christ, and Christ is subject to God. So where a husband's particular decision does not reflect this line of subjection to Christ or is in direct conflict with God's true worship, a woman cannot say she will participate for peace's sake. We seek peace with God first and peace with a man as much as lies with us. This strife is what we call the *offense of the Gospel.* It arises when we stand our ground and say no, out of loyalty to Christ.

Think not that I am come to send peace on earth: I came not to send peace, but a sword.

For I am come to set a man at variance against his father, and the daughter against her mother, and the daughter in law against her mother in law.

And a man's foes shall be they of his own household.

He that loveth father or mother more than me is not worthy of me: and he that loveth son or daughter more than me is not worthy of me.

He that findeth his life, (and we may add his or her marriage) shall lose it: and he that loseth his life for my sake, (and we may also add, he or she that loseth his or her marriage/or my sake) shall find it.

—Matthew 10:34-39

The danger is always when the individual makes a compromise that involves the worship of demons. That is entirely unacceptable. If it causes the unbelieving spouse to depart, then let them leave. As the Scriptures say, "the brother or sister is not bound." But if the unbelieving spouse is willing to dwell with you, without forcing you to commit sacrilege that will offend the Lord, then it is OK, as we have shown above.

We must never forget the Lord's injunction on this matter and the protection that He implied:

And fear not them which kill the body, but are not able to kill the soul: but rather fear him which is able to destroy both soul and body in hell.

Are not two sparrows sold for a farthing? And one of them shall not fall on the ground without your Father.

But the very hairs of your head are all numbered.

Fear ye not, therefore, ye are of more value than many sparrows

—Matthew 10:28-31 (KJV)

He expects us not to fear, but He also expects us to take a bold stand for truth as revealed in His word.

Whosoever therefore shall confess me before men, him will I confess also before my Father which is in heaven.

But whosoever shall deny me before men, him will I also

deny before my Father which is in heaven

—Matthew 10:32-33 (KJV)

It is good to remember that the Christian does not have the right to walk out of the marriage. But if the unbelieving should decide to depart as a result of the conflict, they may leave.

PRACTICAL CHRISTIANITY DIMENSIONS

We have stated earlier that the manifestation of the ninefold Fruit of the Holy Spirit is the sure way of preaching Christ without words. But there are other dimensions.

The Christian in this kind of relationship should not just sit and hope that the unbeliever will be frustrated and depart. Instead, they are under obligation to shine as Light amid the crooked and perverse generation. If the Christian is a woman, the Lord would expect her to submit to her husband and take care of her family, reflecting as much as she possibly can the life of Jesus. The Apostle Peter said as much in his letter to the Church.

Likewise, ye wives, be in subjection to your he own husbands; that, if any obey not the word, they also may without the word be won by the conversation of the wives;

While they behold your chaste conversation coupled with fear.

—1 Peter 3:1-2 (KJV)

I recall some two stories I have read on this. The first one was quite positive and ended with the husband's conversion to Christ. This lady had gone to a women's fellowship meeting, where she gave her life to Jesus. There she also learned about submission to her husband and the care of her home. Hitherto, their home had been one kind of battlefield between husband and wife.

One day the husband came home and was disinclined to wage war on anything. He just decided to stretch out on the sofa. His wife promptly came and helped him remove his shoes, made his meals quickly, and announced that dinner was ready.

His interpretation of her new behavior was that something was the matter with her brain. He was looking for her to snap back to her usual self. But when it persisted, he decided to follow her to acquire it.

The second story is of another lady whose demonstration of Christianity at home was mere sermonizing. She was expecting a house guest for dinner and decided she could step out for a prayer meeting. Meanwhile, the guest arrived, and the dinner wasn't cooked, talk of being ready. Her husband, who was not born again, decided to help out. When she returned, she was not apologetic, but instead blamed her husband for messing up all the lovely ideas she had for the evening.

There is nothing like a seasoned practical Christian life to help an unbelieving spouse see the goodness of the Lord. But this worthwhile effort must be led by the Lord in detail. In Romans chapter 8, verse 14, we read: *As many as are led by the Spirit of God are children of God.* The Lord knows the way to our spouse's salvation. He can get us there faster than we can ever get there ourselves. Therefore, it pays to seek guidance daily as to how we live out our Christian lives practically.

INTERCESSORY PRAYERS

For though we walk in the flesh, we do not war after the flesh: (For the weapons of our warfare are not carnal, but mighty through God to the pulling down of strong-holds;).

Casting down imaginations, and every high thing that exalteth itself against the knowledge of God, and bringing into captivity every thought to the obedience of Christ;

And having in a readiness to revenge all disobedience, when your obedience is fulfilled.

—2 Corinthians 10:3-6

Practical Christianity has a way of energizing and making intercessory prayers more effective. When our obedience is complete in a particular situation, we position ourselves to draw down God's power that causes a man's genuine change. This obedience empowers a person to stop the works of darkness in his or her family.

The Bible declares in Isaiah chapter 10, verse 27, that it is the anointing that breaks the yoke. The prophet Zechariah said as much in chapter 4, verse 6: "*This is the word of the Lord unto Zerubbabel, saying, Not by might, nor by power, but by My Spirit, saith the LORD of hosts.* Obedience to the LORD increases our lives' anointing, which breaks every yoke on us and removes every obstacle on our path.

When we adopt a two-pronged attack such as this, the grace of God overtakes us to make changes that bless our lives. This approach makes this state of one in and one out become two that became one in the Kingdom of God, who are on their way to heaven.

10

THE QUESTIONS THAT REMAIN

INLAWS OBJECTION/PARENTAL CONSENT

The question that arises from this is what a prospective couple should do if their future in-laws reject their proposed union outright. Many churches teach, and rightly too, that prospective couples must obtain parental consent in writing before they agree to solemnize the matrimony. But a potential couple may find this an 'impossible obstacle" to surmount. I believe several options are open to them:

1. Approach the Lord with deep heartfelt intercession to achieve a breakthrough in a dilemma. Today, many married couples would testify that after they fasted and prayed to the Lord, the objecting in-law or in-laws gave their consent.

2. Approach the objecting in-laws with humility and entreaties, striving carefully to explain the basis of your love and proposed union. A concerted effort to break the impasse through the manifestation of the fruit of the Spirit (Galatians 5:22-23) will elicit divine intervention.

Some approaches are unwholesome. One is to threaten to break the relationship before the objecting in-laws. That will suggest a total lack of commitment and will further discourage the objecting in-laws.

3. What should follow the above two measures is the virtue of patience. I recall that our marriage counselor years ago always told us about this prospective couple that waited it out. After about two years of waiting, the lady's parents, who were vehemently opposed, capitulated.

4. Simultaneously, the intending couple should approach the Church's elders to examine the objection and intervene where possible. In some cases, this has been quite effective, particularly when elders of the Church meet with elders of objecting prospective in-laws to share their experiences.

It is still quite possible that all these efforts may prove fruitless. Some would suggest that it may indicate that heaven may not be in support of the union.

I will agree that such a scenario should compel an intending couple to revisit their relationship's foundation. If the review further strengthens their belief in the proposed union, they should approach gifted men of God to examine the matter before the Lord. Sometimes, the objections are mere prejudice or perceptions that bother on stereotypes. If the bias is tribal, ethnic, or racial, the elders of the Church should persevere in their pleas. Stereotypical perceptions may border on past experiences of others who have married people from the same area. For example, some families are vehemently opposed to marriages across denominational divides. If such is the nature of the objections, the elders of the Church who are spiritual should be able to judge the matter before the Lord, to determine the mind of the Lord, bearing in mind Apostle Peter's response to the Jewish leaders in Acts 5:29 where he said: "...We ought to obey God rather than men." Of equal significance is Acts 15:28, which reveals how to judge such a matter: "For it seemed good to the Holy Spirit, and to us, to lay upon you no greater burden than these necessary things..."

It is important to emphasize that the elders should not dismiss the prospective in-laws' objections as baseless but should examine them before the Lord carefully. I have known parental refusals that derive from revelations from the Lord or what I call *spiritual intelligence*. Not too long ago, a lady dropped by my office to narrate very vivid revelations that came to her concerning her son's prospective bride. She fasted and prayed, and the revelations became more explicit with very graphic details, which were confirmed by her son. I invited her son to come and see me for a chat, but he refused. We prayed together, and the lady went away and persisted in her prayers until the young man faced the dangers ahead of him.

There is no doubt that some prospective couples may find these burdens too heavy to bear, as consenting adults under the law do not need parental consent in most societies to sign on the matrimonial dotted line. But the Christian is called to fulfill all righteousness, just as our Lord Jesus Christ did (Matthew 3:13-15). And who knows, some objections may be of the Lord.

THE LEGAL

It is important to note that there are three sides to a marital union. There is the *Legal:* Christian marriages are conducted under the *Ordinance*. The other side is the *traditional wedding,* which requires parental consent. The third dimension is *spiritual,* where the Church solemnizes the union and blesses the couple. Due to constraints like citizenship laws or the domicile of one of the parties, an intending couple may do their court wedding first after obtaining the necessary parental consent. Two visits to the marriage registry will do this; the first to give the mandatory twenty-one days notice for objections and later to sign the register. Christians should always fulfill all the processes so that they can be married according to God's laws, the laws of man, and the culture of the bride.

CASE STUDIES WITHIN MARRIAGE

We now pause to look at different case scenarios found in the Church today to address Christian marriage issues. Here are some examples.

Scenario One:—

The believer (man) who goes to marry an unbeliever (woman)

The details of the case are as follows:

- The man was a believer before the marriage.
- The woman was an unbeliever before the marriage.
- The woman has remained an unbeliever.

What we have established in this study is that marriage for a Christian is a covenant. A believer man who marries an unbeliever woman cannot put her away unless she is unwilling to live with him any longer. In the unfortunate event of fornication, he is expected to forgive and prayerfully love and encourage her to come to Christ. I know a brother who faced this dilemma. He forgave his wife, took her back, and encouraged her to submit her life to Christ. The leeway of fornication as a ground for divorce was essentially for marriages under the law of Moses. In Christ, a man is not allowed to put away his wife in the spirit of 1 Corinthians 7: 11b — "...And let not the husband put away his wife." This no-divorce option is why believers are encouraged to heed the injunction of 2 Corinthians 6:14 before plunging into marriage— "Be not unequally yoked together with unbelievers..."

However, if his wife decides to opt-out of the relationship, the brother's first option should not be to initiate divorce but to ask for the grace to go "the extra mile." He should approach her and her family from whom he married her, with pleas and overtures of reconciliation, as part of his effort to restore the relationship. If the lady's family supports the separation, they would have taken responsibility for breaking the spiritual covenant. They should go further to initiate the legal and customary separation. The brother should not overtly support or encourage such a move. This approach is the path of conscience and the spirit of 1 Corinthians 7:27-28, which says: 'Are you bound to a wife? Do not seek to be loosed. Are you loosed from a wife? Do not seek a wife. 28 But even if you do marry, you have not sinned; and if a virgin marries, she has not sinned. Nevertheless, such will have trouble in the flesh, but I will spare you." (NKJV)

If, after all these efforts, the wife and her family decide to annul the marriage covenant, spiritually, legally, and traditionally, the brother so treated is freed from the relationship in the spirit of 1 Corinthians 7:15: "But if the unbelieving depart, let him depart. A brother or a sister is not under bondage in such cases: but God hath called us to peace."

- Q. What about remarriage under this circumstance?

» Remarriage, as an option for those loosed from their spouse, must always be settled before the Lord. In this peculiar case, because the brother wilfully married an unbeliever against the clear injunction of God's word, he would need time to sort himself out before the Lord. Some Scriptures apply to his situation quite clearly: 1 Corinthians 7:27 and 28, for example: "...Are you loosed from a wife? Do not seek a wife. But even if you do marry, you have not sinned...(NKJV). Some of the others include:(1 Corinthian. 7:7-8) For I would that all men were even as I myself. But every man hath his proper gift of God, one after this manner, and another after that. 8: I say therefore to the unmarried and widows. It is good for them if they abide even as I."

» Besides, the Spirit of the Lord may constrain the brother so long as the sister has not remarried, which keeps the door of reconciliation open. Such a constraint would indicate that the Lord is still at work on the matter, and any move that is contrary to that constraint would be further complicating matters spiritually. No Christian should ever forget that the spiritual controls the physical always. What is decided in heaven determines what should happen on earth, as revealed in Revelations chapter 3, verse 7: And to the angel of the Church in Philadelphia write; These things saith He that is holy, He that is true, He that hath the key of David, he that openeth, and no man shutteth; and shutteth, and no man openeth. No Christian in his or her right spiritual senses should put himself or herself on a collision course with the Spirit of the Lord.

Barring such a constraint, such a brother may opt to stay celibate and chaste for a long time or the rest of his life. What is more likely, though, is that his passions and the need for companionship would sooner than later get the better of him. The apostle has cautioned that it is better to marry than to burn. Worse still, it is better to marry than to get involved in secret sins of fornication, adultery, masturbation, and the like. No one should mortgage his spiritual life to a constant self condemnatory charge of hypocrisy.

Scenario Two:-

The believer (woman) who is married to an unbeliever (man)

The details of the case are as follows:

- ★ The woman was a believer before the marriage
- ★ The man was an unbeliever before the marriage
- ★ The man has remained an unbeliever

This situation is quite similar to the case discussed above. The lady married the man against the clear injunction of God's word. It is important to note that such a woman is:

★ Bound to her husband as long as he is alive, in the spirit of 1 Corinthians 7:39 and Romans 7:1-3.

★ She is not allowed to depart from her husband for any reason, 1 Corinthians 7:10

★ The husband may depart, but she cannot in conscience file for formal separation. For, part of the repentance and restitution called for here, as in scenario one above, is a determination to do all in one's power by way of sacrifice and godliness to bring the other party to the saving knowledge of Jesus Christ. This attitude was what the Apostle Peter had in mind in 1 Peter 3:1-2: "Likewise, ye wives, be in subjection to your own husbands; that, if any obey not the word, they also may without the word be won by the conversation of the wives; While they behold your chaste conversation coupled with fear."

» However, were this to fail, and the husband insists on leaving the marital home, the sister must continue patiently to intercede for him, while making use of the godly counsel of elders in the Church and the family to pursue the path of reconciliation. If the husband were to remarry, he put the final nail on the coffin of the marriage covenant in the spirit of Deuteronomy 24:1-4. Such a move by the husband would free the sister from the bonds of the relationship. Her family has a moral right to insist that he grant her a formal separation similar to Moses' formal letter of divorce.

- Concerning remarriage, the injunctions in 1 Corinthians 7:27-28 will apply, in the spirit of the Scripture in Galatians 3:28, which says that men and women are one in Christ.

Scenario Three:—

The unbeliever (man or woman) that had married before either of them became a believer.

Let us note the details of the case clearly:

- The man was an unbeliever before the marriage
- The woman was an unbeliever before the marriage
- One of them got converted after the marriage, thereby creating a scenario similar to scenarios 1 and 2 above.

The brother or sister should believe that the grace of God that brought him/her to Christ will also bring his or her spouse. It may take time. It may take a great deal of pain, suffering, patience, humility, and the same virtues of the fruit of the Holy Spirit. But those who persevere in faith end up becoming overcomers with a testimony to God's glory.

» (i) 1 Corinthians 7:12-13 is the relevant scripture to apply. So, if your wife is an unbeliever, but she is happy, married to you, you should continue to love and cherish her.

» (ii) If your husband is an unbeliever, and he is happy to live with you, you should continue to submit to him and to honor him in the spirit of Ephesians 5:22-24

» (iii). We should note that this is vital to the covering of the children spiritually. The Bible recognizes that Christian parents that have the Spirit of God in them provide spiritual cover for their children. So, no man or woman who is a Christian should lightly abandon children to unbelieving spouses in the spirit of 1 Corinthians 7:14. By staying in the marriage, you help provide spiritual cover for all the family.

IN SEARCH OF A NEW BONE OF MY BONES

» (i) It is clear that there is no Biblical support for those who teach that a Christian convert, (male or female) should abandon his/her wife/husband of many years and pick up another sister/brother who is now supposedly the real bone of his bones and flesh of his flesh.

» (ii) It is good to state quite categorically that this teaching is false for the following reasons:

- a. The Bible teaches that marriage is a covenant made with the author of marriage, God Almighty, the third party, or the faithful witness.

- b. Once a person has entered into the covenant, then he or she cannot just simply opt out in the spirit of Matthew 19:8-9 quoted earlier. This passage of Scripture is a blanket statement that covers all marriages outside of grace.

» (iii) There are those who argue that since it was not God who joined them together, having married as unbelievers, they are at liberty to put the relationship asunder. It is difficult to sustain such an argument in truth and conscience. If a Christian is having difficulties with integration in his/her marriage, what is called for is a greater development of Christ's mind, not a seeming loophole to obtain a divorce. We must all be careful to be seen and heard doing nothing against the truth but for the truth (2 Corinthians 13:8).

» (iv). It is essential for us not to give heed to seducing spirits, which are determined to create confusion in the Church, which is Christ's body. A teaching like this can unleash the monster of lust in the body of Christ, that can tear families apart while lusting mates laden with many sins (2 Timothy 3:6-7) but pretending to be spiritual, go after other peoples wives and children, leading to utter chaos in the Church. Luke 17:1 -2 is an ample warning for all those who cause young converts to stumble in their faith.

» (v) The unbeliever in the relationship may object to the newfound faith in Christ of his or her spouse. If he or she decides to opt-out as a result, according to 1 Corinthians 7:15, the spouse so deserted is not bound. However, having been both unbelievers before, the brother or sister must be patient. The way to handle it is to intercede for the spouses' salvation, not to pursue separation.

Scenario Four:—

Two unbelievers that got married before they both became believers

The details are as follows:

- ★ The man was an unbeliever before the marriage
- ★ The woman was an unbeliever before the marriage
- ★ Both of them are now converted

As the two have become believers, they are now under grace both of them, and separation is ruled out entirely in the spirit of 1 Corinthians 7:10-11. *And unto the married I command, yet not I, but the Lord, Let not the wife depart from her husband: But and if she depart, let her remain unmarried, or be reconciled to her husband: and let not the husband put away his wife.*

Scenario Five:—

Single or widowed unbeliever (man) that married a divorced (unbeliever) woman before the (man's) conversion

The details are as follows:

- ★ The man was single or widowed before the marriage
- ★ The woman was divorced
- ★ They got married as unbelievers
- ★ The man got converted after the marriage
- ★ The woman is still an unbeliever

» (i) As we can see clearly from the previous discussions, this is a marriage conducted outside of the appropriation of God's grace. Therefore, the wife's separation and remarriage have invalidated the covenants of her previous marriage in the spirit of Deuteronomy 24:1-4. She can no longer return to her last husband, who may have remarried too.

» (ii) The situation is therefore similar to Scenario one and two, where a believer is married to an unbeliever.

» (iii) The principles enunciated in 1 Corinthians 7:10-15 is what should apply here. If the lady is willing to dwell with the brother, then he should not put her away.

» (iv) The challenge posed in verse 16, should inspire the man to pray earnestly for the salvation of his wife: 16: *For what knowest thou, O wife, whether thou shalt save thy husband? Or how knowest thou, O man, whether thou shalt save thy wife?*

» (v) If the woman decides to opt-out of the marriage because the man has surrendered his life to Christ, then the brother or sister is not bound. It is the unbeliever that departed and in the spirit of 1 Corinthians 7:15, the brother or sister is not bound.

Scenario Six:—

Single or widowed unbeliever (woman) that got married to a divorced (unbeliever) man before the (woman's) conversion

The details are as follows:

- ★ The woman was single or widowed before the marriage
- ★ The man was divorced
- ★ They got married as unbelievers
- ★ The woman got converted after the marriage
- ★ The man is still an unbeliever

We must note that Scenarios five and six are quite similar. One is the converse of the other. The five points of Scenario 5 above should, therefore, apply here as well.

Scenario Seven:—

Two divorcees (man and woman) who got married before their conversion

The details are as follows:

- ★ The man was divorced before the marriage
- ★ The woman was also divorced before the marriage
- ★ They got married as unbelievers
- ★ They both got converted after their marriage

» (i) In line with our previous case discussions, remarriage invalidates the bond of marriage according to (Deuteronomy 24:1-4). They cannot, therefore, return to their former relationships.

» (ii) Their case is, therefore, similar to two Christians who are married.

» (iii). There is no room for divorce or remarriage among two Christians (1 Corinthians. 7:10-11).

» (iv) The grace of God and the fruit and power of the Holy Spirit should help them keep their union until the end.

Scenario Eight:—

Two divorcees (man and woman) who are contemplating marriage after their conversion

The details are as follows:

- ★ The man has been divorced from his wife as an unbeliever
- ★ The woman has been divorced from her husband as an unbeliever
- ★ Both of them are now believers

- ★ They are contemplating marriage but have not yet married

Because neither of them has remarried, the issues have become somewhat conditional. A few questions arise:

- 1. Where are the man's former wife and the woman's former husband?

- 2. Has either or both remarried?

- 3. Has either or both become Christians?

- 4. Is either of them that has not remarried willing to take his/her spouse back?

» (i) Here are the key facts here: One of the spouses has become a Christian and has not remarried. The brother or sister is bound in conscience to seek reconciliation, rather than jump on to a new relationship.

» (ii) If none of the spouses has become Christian, but they are willing to have their husband or wife back, the wife or husband in question should return to his/her family, rather than jump on to a new relationship. Again this will be the path of conscience in the spirit of 1 Corinthians 7:12-13. *But to the rest speak I, not the Lord: If any brother hath a wife that believeth not, and she be pleased to dwell with him, let him not put her away. And the woman which hath an husband that believeth not, and if he be pleased to dwell with her, let her not leave him.*

» (iii) If neither of them has remarried, but none is willing to have the spouses back, the Christian must carefully seek the mind of God. The path of conscience in the spirit of God's word would be to intercede for the spouse's change of heart now that one has become a Christian.

It is not to jump at the opportunity of a new relationship. I am quite confident that where this is done earnestly and sincerely in the integrity of one's heart, the Spirit of the Lord will intervene one way or another. So long as the former spouse has not remarried, one should pursue the reconciliation path with prayerful vigor—the help of pastors and elders who should judge the circumstances before the Lord must be solicited.

» (iv). The elders of the Church may intervene if neither of the spouses outside the proposed union is willing to have his/her wife or husband back. Under such circumstances, they should be able to grant the parties to the proposed union leave to marry in the spirit of 1 Corinthians 6:2-3: *Do ye not know that the saints shall judge the world? And if the earth shall be judged by you, are ye unworthy to judge the smallest matters? Know ye not that we shall judge angels? How much more things that pertain to this life?* Their divorce from their previous marriages may be judged as "Times of Ignorance" in the spirit of Acts 17:30

» (v) This decision by the elders saves the brother and sister from the temptation of fornication, which the Bible greatly deplores. The elders must, therefore, act in love, trying as much as possible to put themselves in the shoes of the brother and the sister, who have tried earnestly to seek reconciliation with their spouses over a significant period, always remembering the spirit of 1 Corinthians 7:2, which says: *Nevertheless, to avoid fornication, let every man have his own wife, and let every woman have her own husband.* The Bible says in 1 Corinthians 7:35 that there is a need for us to serve the Lord without distraction. *And this I speak for your own profit; not that I may cast a snare upon you, but for that which is comely, and that ye may attend upon the Lord without distraction.*

» (vi) The elders must, however, judge each case in isolation before the Lord, seeking to elicit what the mind of the Lord is in every situation. It might be possible that the Lord might allow one intending couple to go ahead and marry while constraining another. Each individual must seek to act in conscience before the Lord of all heaven and earth. There is a principle in discipleship that says: *"others may, but you can't.'* This is how the Spirit of the Lord isolates us for the work He has for us as individuals. The Apostle Paul spoke about such isolation in 1 Corinthians 9:5: *Do we have no right to take along a believing wife, as do the other apostles, the brothers of the Lord and Cephas?*

» We must note though that no brother or sister should attempt illegality and enter another relationship when a previous one has not been annulled. Even when an unbelieving partner has departed, a proper bill of divorce must be issued to avoid breaking the law of the land.

Scenario Nine:—

Two divorcees (man and woman) who have gotten married after their conversion

- ★ The man has been divorced from his wife as an unbeliever
- ★ The woman has been divorced from her husband as an
    - o unbeliever
- ★ Both of them are now believers
- ★ They have gone ahead to marry in court
- ★ The couple had already married, so the above points cannot apply as their remarriage has invalidated their previous marriages in the spirit of Deuteronomy 24:1-4. However, suppose the Church should find out that their marriage was

done preemptively as a fait accompli, mainly because either of their previous spouses had been converted and had been yearning for reconciliation and the couple was aware of it? In that case, such a move should be condemned openly in the spirit of 1 Timothy 5:20: *Them that sin rebuke before all, that others also may fear.* The discipleship program for intending couples of all categories should help spell out the Church's position.

Scenario Ten:—

Divorced converts, who marry single or widowed Christians after their conversion

The details are as follows:

* The man/woman was divorced from his/her spouse as an unbeliever
* He/she is now converted
* He/she plans to marry a single/widowed brother or sister

This case is similar to scenarios eight and nine above but not identical. The difference here is that only one party has a previous relationship to sort out in the light of God's word.

» The separated brother/sister should establish the following concerning his/her previous relationship.

- 1. Where is his/her spouse now? They must try and locate them.

- 2. Has he/she become a Christian too?

- 3. Has he/she remarried?

- 4. Are they willing to be reconciled to their spouse?

(i) If the spouse in question has remained unmarried and has become a Christian, every effort should be made to reconcile the two parties. Because they have both become Christians, they should study the word of God that clearly states that believers in Christ should not separate from their spouses (1 Corinthians. 7:10-11). There should be a call for mutual forgiveness, mutual repentance, and the restoration of trust through faith in God. As the prophet Isaiah said, in Isaiah 1:18, we have an open invitation to come and reason together with the Lord about our past. Those who heed this call of the Lord discover the Lord's hand that is laden with blessings for those who trust and obey Him.

» (ii) The key facts are: The spouse of the brother or sister in question has remarried or has remained an unbeliever. Secondly, they are unwilling to be reconciled. Then the brother or sister is not bound, in the spirit of 1 Corinthians 7:15

Scenario Eleven:—

Divorced believer—a man (converted after remarriage) married to a divorced unbeliever woman.

The details are as follows:

- ★ The man was divorced from a previous relationship
- ★ His wife was also divorced from a previous relationship
- ★ They both married as unbelievers.
- ★ The man got converted after the second marriage.
- ★ The woman is still an unbeliever

» (i) As has been previously discussed, the fact of remarriage has invalidated the bonds of the two previous relationships in the spirit of Deuteronomy 24:1-4.

» (ii) Because the brother is now a believer, the injunction of 1 Corinthians 7:12-13 will apply as previously discussed under scenarios one and two.

Scenario Twelve:—

Divorced believer—a woman (converted after remarriage) married to a divorced unbeliever man.

The details are as follows:

* The woman was divorced from a previous relationship
* Her husband was also divorced from a previous relationship
* They both married as unbelievers.
* The woman got converted after the second marriage.
* The man is still an unbeliever

This situation is the converse of scenario eleven above. The same solution should, therefore, apply.

OTHER MARRIAGE QUESTIONS

Scenario Thirteen:—

A single man (believer) who put a single girl (unbeliever) in the family way

The details are as follows:

* The man is single and of marriageable age
* He is a believer in a backslidden state who committed fornication
* The girl in question is pregnant and is an unbeliever

This scenario is a clear case of walking in a disorderly manner in the body of Christ. The Church must be at the forefront of cleaning its own house. The children of God must walk according to the truth of the Word of God.

Now we command you, brethren, in the name of our Lord Jesus Christ, that ye withdraw yourselves from every brother that walketh disorderly, and not after the tradition which he received of us. 7: For yourselves know how ye ought to follow us: for we behaved not ourselves disorderly among you;
—2 Thessalonians 3:6-7

There is the path of honor and responsibility, which the Bible recommends in Deuteronomy 22:28-29.

If a man find a damsel that is a virgin, which is not betrothed, and lay hold on her, and lie with her, and they be found; 29: Then the man that lay with her shall give unto the damsel's father fifty shekels of silver, and she shall be his wife; because he hath humbled her, he may not put her away all his days.

This passage of Scripture provides the only path of honor and righteousness in this matter. Some argue that since the girl is not a believer, the man should not marry her as she could not possibly be "bone of his bones and flesh of his flesh." Such a point is somewhat belated, and the Church should prevail on the brother to marry the lady. Besides, every effort must be made to prevent the birth of children who will have all kinds of traumatic identity crises.

16: And if a man entice a maid that is not betrothed, and lie with her, he shall surely endow her to be his wife. 17: If her father utterly refuse to give her unto him, he shall pay money according to the dowry of virgins.

—Exodus 22:16-17

The exception to this counsel should be where the father of the girl refuses to accept the man. I believe that where the Lord disapproves of the union, He might use the girl's family to say so, that the Scriptures may not be broken.

Scenario Fourteen:—

A single man (unbeliever) who put a single girl (believer) in the family way

The details are as follows:

- ⋆ The man is single and of marriageable age
- ⋆ The girl involved is a believer in a backslidden state
- ⋆ The girl has become pregnant
- ⋆ » The girl, in this case, is also walking disorderly and must follow the path of repentance and restitution. Some counsel that a Christian man is more likely to bring his unbeliever wife to Church. A Christian girl with a husband who is an unbeliever has a more challenging time. Again these considerations are somewhat belated, and generally, the Bible injunctions cited above should prevail. However, if the unbeliever man is unwilling to marry the girl, then she and her family must protect the child and take care of him/her as much as is practicable under the circumstances. There is no room for abortion to cover sin in the body of Christ.

Scenario Fifteen:—

A married man (believer) who put a single girl (unbeliever) in the family way

The details are as follows:

- ★ The man is married and a believer
- ★ He is in a backslidden state and involved in the sin of adultery
- ★ The girl involved is pregnant and is an unbeliever

The severity with which the Bible views adultery cases is seen in the prescribed punishment.

10: And the man that committeth adultery with another man's wife, even he that committeth adultery with his neighbor's wife, the adulterer and the adulteress shall surely be put to death.
—Leviticus 20:10

» (i) The Church must therefore put the brother under discipline in the light of 1 Corinthians 5:1-7:

1: I can hardly believe the report about the sexual immorality going on among you, something so evil that even the pagans don't do it. I am told that you have a man in your Church who is living in sin with his father's wife. 2: And you are so proud of yourselves! Why aren't you mourning in sorrow and shame? And why haven't you removed this man from your fellowship? 3: Even though I am not there with you in person, I am with you in the spirit. Concerning the one who has done this, I have already passed judgment: in the name of the Lord Jesus. You are to call a meeting of the Church, and I will be there in spirit, and the power of the Lord Jesus will be with you as you meet then you must cast this man out of the Church and into Satan's hands, so that his sinful nature will be destroyed and he himself will be saved when the Lord returns. How terrible that you should boast about your spirituality, and yet you let this sort of thing go on. Don't you realize that if even one person is allowed to go on sinning, soon all will be affected? 7: Remove this wicked person from among you so that you can stay pure...(NLT)

» (ii) If adultery and fornication appear to be widespread among the believers, then the leaders should adopt open rebuke to stamp it out as recommended in 1 Timothy 5:20. *Anyone who sins should be rebuked in front of the whole Church so that others will have a proper fear of God.* (NLT). This style of rebuke is to make it abundantly clear to all that sexual immorality is incompatible with spirituality and that God Almighty would have the Church stamp it out where ever it exists.

» (iii) The process of discipline is designed to produce repentance and correction as detailed below.

» (iv) A proper restitution must be made to the girl's family in the spirit of Deuteronomy 22:28-29, which says that a man that seduces a young lady must pay the dowry to her parents and marry her, and must not put her away for life. However, because the man is already married, such an option would not be tenable as the Church does not allow polygamy. Therefore, his restitution should center on a proper financial arrangement to take care of the lady until she marries. Concerning the baby, quite a few options exist. The man and his wife can take up the child if the girl and her family agree. Alternatively, the girl can decide to raise her child with financial support from the man. The other alternative is to put up the child for adoption by mutual consent.

» (v) It must be repeatedly made clear that adultery breaks the marriage covenant, and only the grace of God can restore love to a relationship where the bed has been defiled. The Lord will judge such acts among believers severely, as taught in the Bible.

Marriage is honorable in all, and the bed undefiled: but whoremongers and adulterers God will judge.

—Hebrews 13:4)

» (vi) A Christian should, therefore, confess such a fault to his wife in full repentance in the spirit of James 5:16 *Confess your faults one to another, and pray one for another, that ye may be healed. The effectual fervent prayer of a righteous man availeth much.*

Scenario Sixteen:—

A married man (unbeliever) who put a single girl (believer) in the family way

The details are as follows:

- ⋆ The man is married and an unbeliever
- ⋆ The girl though a believer is in a backslidden state and has committed adultery
- ⋆ The girl has become pregnant.

» This is the converse of scenario fourteen above, so all the things discussed above would apply except that the Christian has minimal control over how an unbeliever conducts his affairs. Such a girl must repent before the Lord and earnestly ask the Lord for forgiveness and restoration. It should be possible to make the same arrangements as outlined above for the girl and her child's upkeep. Her natural family and Church family must intervene from the beginning, as they would invariably provide the bulk of the long term support she would need for her spiritual and psychological rehabilitation.

Scenario Seventeen:—

A single man (believer) who put a single girl (believer) in the family way

The details are as follows:

- ⋆ The man and the woman are both believers and of marriageable age
- ⋆ Both are in a backslidden state and committed fornication
- ⋆ The girl is pregnant

(i) This is the case scenario that the Bible says should not be mentioned among believers in Christ.

3: But fornication, and all uncleanness, or covetousness, let it not be once named among you, as becometh saints;

—Ephesians 5:3

» (ii) It is crucial here that individual churches should have their way of putting the brother and the sister under discipline in the spirit of 1 Corinthians. 5:1-7. Public exposure may not always be the best solution, but there is a need for a deterrent sanction to forewarn others. The Spirit of God must always lead one to the best way to aid genuine repentance and restoration in the spirit of Galatians 6:1. *Dear brothers and sisters, if some sin overcomes another Christian, you who are godly should gently and humbly help that person back onto the right path. And be careful not to fall into the same temptation yourself. (NLT)*

» (iii) The objective is, therefore, to correct the brother and the sister by bringing them to true repentance, as also happened in the Church at Corinth. (2 Corinthians. 2:6-11,7:8-12)

» (iv) Those who resist discipline should be ex-communicated from the Church in the spirit of 1 Corinthians 5:11

» (v) The Church should always encourage such people to go ahead and get married since they are both believers. That should be the path of honor and responsibility advocated in God's word (Deuteronomy 22:28-29).

Scenario Eighteen:—

A single man (believer) guilty of "progressive sampling" of single ladies

The details are as follows:

- The man is single and of marriageable age
- The sisters he has gone to bed with are single and of
    - marriageable age
- The man has refused to marry any of them

» (i) Any brother who commits fornication with several sisters must be put under severe discipline and closely monitored in the Church. He is a danger to the spiritual health of the body of Christ to which he belongs. He must not be allowed to hold any responsibility whatsoever in the Church, particularly ones that may expose him directly to members of the opposite sex until the unclean spirit (s) that appear to control his life is exorcised. The same measures will apply to a sister known to be seducing young men in the Church.

» (ii) If it is a minister or pastor in an organization that is involved, then it becomes necessary to handle it at the highest level. The Church must preserve its moral authority in society and also set a very high standard of morality that does not mislead or confuse the people in the spirit of Matthew 18:6-7. *But if anyone causes one of these little ones who trusts in me to lose faith, it would be better for that person to be thrown into the sea with a large millstone tied around the neck. 7: How terrible it will be for anyone who causes others to sin. The temptation to do wrong is inevitable, but how terrible it will be for the person who does the tempting. (NLT)*

» (iii). If the sinner is the pastor/founder, then his/her board of elders must step in with firmness to help the minister recover his/her moral integrity and authority. A time of seclusion should be followed by ardent intercession by all the members of his congregation. I know of a Church where the board of elders never allowed their pastor to counsel a member of the opposite sex alone as a precautionary measure. They would insist that the door to the room must be left open, and a member of the board of elders must be waiting in an ante-room as a chaperone. I felt that it was a mature way of dealing with the problem while it lasted.

» (iv). The brother must be made to see the virtue of 1 Corinthians 7:2. But because there is so much sexual immorality, each man should have his own wife, and each woman should have her own husband. Where he fails to settle down quickly enough but continues to behave like "a wolf in sheep's clothing, "then he must be suspended from the Church entirely. A counselor told me the other day that a young man in their Church ravaged the single girls in his Church arm, (workgroup within the Church) and ruined their reputation and Christian testimony. He always warmed his way into their hearts with promises of marriage, which never materialized. The relationships usually ended soon after one or two sessions of sex. The pastor had to denounce him openly from the pulpit to protect his flock and Christ's name. That forced him to withdraw from the Church.

» (v). One must emphasize that the sisters so seduced must have themselves to blame as well, as they should know that the Lord expects them to keep their virtue in Christ intact until their honeymoon night. This truth must be emphasized again and again in Church. To have men and women of easy virtue parading around in Church as believers must speak to us all in the body of Christ about what the future would look like unless we establish old fashioned morality and purity among the people of God.

MARRIAGE EXPECTATIONSAMONG BELIEVERS

The position that has been taken in this book is that marriage among believers is forever. I did state that not even fornication should be an irrevocable ground for divorce in the light of Luke 17:3: *Take heed to yourselves: If thy brother trespass against thee, rebuke him; and if he repent, forgive him.* Again the Prophet Malachi stated quite categorically that the Lord hates putting away (Malachi 2:16).

This position pre-supposes that you are dealing with a Christian who overtaken in a fault, according to Galatians 6:1-2:

Brethren, if a man be overtaken in a fault, ye which are spiritual, restore such an one in the spirit of meekness; considering thyself, lest thou also be tempted. 2: Bear ye one another's burdens, and so fulfill the law of Christ.

But if what you are dealing with is a fake member, who is purely a fornicator and an enemy of the cross of Christ, then the matter would call for re-examination in the spirit of Philippians 3:17. *Brethren, be followers together of me and mark them which walk so as ye have us for an ensample.* The same thought is established by 1 Corinthians 5:11. *What I meant was that you are not to associate with anyone who claims to be a Christian yet indulges in sexual sin, or is greedy, or worships idols, or is abusive, or a drunkard, or a swindler. Don't even eat with such people (NLT).*

NEED FOR TEMPORARY SEPARATION

What the Bible is saying in 1 Corinthians 5:11 calls for closer scrutiny. This kind of withdrawal advocated here is to show the severest form of disapproval. When a supposed brother or sister persists in sin, is resistant to God's word and the council of elders in the Church, he leaves the Church no alternative but to apply measures to enforce discipline and change. The Bible is quite clear on what should be done under the circumstances.

15: Moreover, if thy brother shall trespass against thee, go and tell him his fault between thee and him alone: if he shall hear thee, thou hast gained thy brother. 16: But if he will not hear thee, then take with thee one or two more, that in the mouth of two or three witnesses every word may be established. 17: And if he shall neglect to hear them, tell it unto the Church: but if he neglect to hear the Church, let him be unto thee as an heathen man and a publican.

—Matthew 18:15-17

This Scripture provides the basis for sanctions of erring brethren within the Church and should be applied without respect of persons so that the Church of the living God will continue to be the pillar and ground of the truth (1 Timothy 3:15).

Some of the grounds listed for sanctions are as follows:

Fornicator

That would not just be overtaken in a fault once and has repented, as devastating and shocking as this must be to a Christian spouse who naturally would feel betrayed. The Greek word translated fornicator in the passage of Scripture is *pornos* from which we get the word pornography. The Bible is speaking of sexual debasement, male harlotry, or a whoremonger. If a supposed Christian husband or wife is suffering from a virulent form of sexual incontinence, associated with a total breakdown of all control, the Bible recommends dissociation. Whether this will be temporary or go on to become permanent will depend on his/her willingness to repent and make restitution. An unclean spirit may oppress such a person, and where they are willing, other brethren in the Church should assist them with counseling, followed by the casting out of the unclean spirits that might be plaguing him or her.

23 Suddenly there was a man in their synagogue who had an unclean spirit. He screamed,

24 "What do you want with us, Jesus of Nazareth? Have you come to destroy us? I know who you are—the Holy One of God!"

25 But Jesus reprimanded him, saying, "Be quiet, and come out of him!"

26 At this, the unclean spirit shook the man, cried out with a loud voice, and came out of him.

—*Mark 1:23-26 (ISV)*

Idolater

Idolatry is one sin that angers God and provokes His jealousy. The Bible is quite clear on this:

For thou shalt worship no other god: for the LORD, whose name is Jealous, is a jealous God:

—Exodus 34:14

A supposed brother or sister that is an idolater risks the lives of all the family. The jealousy of the Lord burns like a fire, the Bible says. Nobody should take things for granted.

21: They have moved me to jealousy with that which is not God; they have provoked me to anger with their vanities: and I will move them to jealousy with those which are not a people; I will provoke them to anger with a foolish nation.
—Deuteronomy 32:21

If a brother or sister continues to worship idols or consult demons, the Bible recommends dissociation to pave the way for repentance and restitution.

Such a brother or sister should be under discipline in the Church no matter how highly placed in society or how much money they bring to the Church.

Railer

The Greek word used here is *ioidoros*, meaning abusive. In other words, when a marriage has become abusive, with physical violence and injury, the Bible recommends dissociation. Husbands who turn their wives into punching bags must know that the Bible instructs dissociation. To presume that the woman bound to her husband by the law of the spirit will tolerate the physical violence and not attempt to leave is tragic and inhuman. The Bible clearly says that such a brother or sister should be under discipline in the Church no matter how highly placed in society or how much money they bring to the Church.

Drunkard

The Greek word here is *methusk*, which means to intoxicate or to be drunk. What the Bible says here is clear. If a brother is always drunk and not in control and refuses to submit to therapy and change, he should know that the Church has a right to put him under discipline and withdraw from him if he persists. Alcoholism invariably leads to violence, with battering. Rather than ruin the whole family through alcoholism and violence, some dissociation recommended here may serve to jolt him to his senses. The whole idea here is that Christians should not take their spouses for granted on the premise that they are stuck with them. Love and a high sense of responsibility will make all these unnecessary. But the Bible offers some respite for those who are choked to death by brethren who are fornicators, railers, drunkards, and extortioners.

Extortioner

The Greek word here is *harpax*, meaning extortion, ravening, plundering, someone who lives through extortion. The Bible says that if a brother is known to be an extortioner, he should be under discipline in the Church. In Nigeria today, this is generally referred to as the '419 scams." I know pastors who would like to see the source of your income if you bring them an unusually large tithe or offering, over and above your usual level of giving. Admittedly, their churches may not be rolling in money, but they are preparing their congregations for

God's kingdom rather than the kingdom of men. A brother or sister may dissociate, albeit temporarily, from a relationship if the spouse, who is supposed to be a Christian, is an extortioner. He or she should ask the Church to intervene and bring the erring brother or sister to repentance.

Summary

The Bible counsels us to work out our salvation with fear and trembling (Philippians 2:12). Families should be run in love and the fear of God so that Christians will indeed be light to their generation in each generation.

This temporary dissociation is designed to produce repentance and correction and not to break-up the relationship. It is not to be a prelude to divorce. It is merely to allow space and time to sort out what the Bible has treated as fundamental flaws in the spiritual orientation that can derail the journey through life to God's Kingdom. Therefore, it must be contemplated carefully under the Holy Spirit's guidance so that it will produce fruit unto righteousness. The Spirit of God will not allow it where it will hinder rather than help. It is good to involve the elders of the Church, for this is the teaching of Scripture in Matt. 18:15-17. By involving elders, we provide help and support to oppressed, abused, and battered people in "Christian homes."

REMARRIAGE

It is crucial to address this question once and for all to put it in perspective. Some teach that a Christian separated from a marriage should remain single. The word of God does not support that position:

I suppose therefore that this is good for the present distress, I say, that it is good for a man so to be. 27: Art thou bound unto a wife? seek not to be loosed. Art thou loosed from a wife? seek not a wife. 28: But and if thou marry, thou hast not sinned; and if a virgin marry, she hath not sinned. Nevertheless such shall have trouble in the flesh: but I spare you.

—1 Corinthians 7:26-28 (KJV)

A Christian loosed from a marriage relationship should marry if he cannot contain, to avoid fornication. We must note that the sin of fornication has grave implications for a person's spiritual life.

1*: Now concerning the things of which ye wrote unto me: It is good for a man not to touch a woman. 2: Nevertheless, to avoid fornication, let every man have his own wife, and let every woman have her own husband.*

—1 Corinthians 7:1-2

18: Flee fornication. Every sin that a man doeth is without the body; but he that committeth fornication sinneth against his own body. 19: What? Know ye not that your body is the temple of the Holy Ghost which is in you, which ye have of God, and ye are not your own?

20: For ye are bought with a price: therefore glorify God in your body, and in your spirit, which are God's.

—1 Corinthians 6:18-20

3: For this is the will of God, even your sanctification, that ye should abstain from fornication:

4: That every one of you should know how to possess

his vessel in sanctification and honor;

5: Not in the lust of concupiscence, even as the Gentiles which know not God:

—1 Thessalonians. 4:3-5

I have encountered many young men and women who were victims of a horrible marital experience. I know a young man whose wife was granted divorce by the court and also given custody of their children. She was already living with another man at the time. She went on to marry the man and to raise another family. His counselor told the young man that he could not take another wife. I did not find a Biblical basis for such a counsel because his wife's infidelity had invalidated their marriage vow. His wife was not seeking forgiveness. She had remarried, and so the brother could no longer take her back in the spirit of Deuteronomy 24:1-4. It was evident that the brother was being driven out of the Church or sometimes out of the faith because I could not see him living the rest of his life, single and chaste.

The remarriage of his spouse should put a seal or closure on the previous marriage, and the brother or sister so loosed from the relationship should be free to remarry if he or she cannot contain. Remarriage is always better than secret acts of fornication or adultery, or any form of self-abuse.

POLYGAMY

This subject has been dealt with extensively in chapter 8, under the leadership qualities in the Church. A Bishop, the Bible says, must be the husband of one wife.

I believe those of us who minister owe it to God and the body of Christ to study these issues and prayerfully take a stand. The Church of Jesus

Christ should have a firm moral and spiritual voice in society, helping societies overcome initial obstacles on their way to evolving truly Bible-based Christian communities.

Thus, the door will be open for people born into other cultures and other religions that practice polygamy to embrace the faith and find a place for growth and maturity in the body of Christ. So long as we invite people to come to Christ as they are, we must be careful to handle constraints that do not bear directly on spirituality or godliness. That will create the flexibility we need to accommodate new converts to Christ from other religions where polygamy is permitted.

We know that the LORD may constrain some to disengage from polygamous relationships and stay by themselves. But coming from a polygamous marriage into Christ should not scatter the home as some teach. Such converts should grow in the Lord and serve their Lord and their God with joy and without condemnation. They do not need to be pastors, elders, or deacons.

I recall a visit to a church here in Nigeria where the pastor confided that a particular convert to Christianity had not been able to bring his two wives to Church because certain elders had told him to wait. The pastor did not wish to contradict his elders, and so he asked my opinion. I promptly pointed out to him that God saves us as we are. A man with two wives coming from another faith/religion was saved with his household by the Lord. The least the Church should do is welcome them all with open arms and allow them room to grow in the Lord. This is the one way to encourage people of other faiths and cultures to come to Christ. But if coming to Christ for them would mean disrupting their family relationships, and turning wives and children to the streets, many will be discouraged.

New converts to Christianity, therefore, in polygamous relationships before their conversion, must be given room to be led by the Lord. Our Lord Jesus Christ had told us clearly that He is the one to build His Church (Matthew 16:18). All we have to do is continue to teach principles of godliness in love while allowing the Spirit of the Lord to define each individual's path in life. God is the final judge of all things, including these matters that ante-date one's conversion, ostensibly done in ignorance.

11

MEETING SPECIAL NEEDS IN MARRIAGE

A book on marriage, written or reviewed in this time and age, will be incomplete if it fails to mention some families' peculiar needs. This need has to do with having children or with the gender of their children. Questions have also arisen about single parenthood by choice, particularly for aging ladies who have not managed to tie the knot with someone but would like to have a child of their own.

Infertility

Scientific and technological advancement have tackled the infertility challenges of quite a diverse spectrum of couples. There is the common practice of in-vitro fertilization - IVF, with sperm and egg belonging to the couple. This procedure has resulted in many couples having children of their own with great relief and joy. As with most of these modern ways of alleviating the scourge of infertility, the couple must be in a position to decide for themselves. The widespread paternity check is there to ensure that the laboratory did not switch eggs or sperms. Medical Centres that do IVF should have a reputation to protect and should therefore ensure that such mix-ups don't occur.

Infertility using donor sperm or egg

The few people who ask about this receive the standard answer I usually give: this is similar to adoption. There is no direct Bible reference on which to base a decision on this question; the individual is therefore left to his/her conscience before the LORD. It is vital to say that no one should base such a decision on another's perspective. There are two Scriptures, in my opinion, that can assist the individual in making his/her decision. The first is in **2 Corinthians 5:9-10 (NLT2)**

9 So whether we are here in this body or away from this body, our goal is to please him.

10 For we must all stand before Christ to be judged. We will each receive whatever we deserve for the good or evil we have done in this earthly body.

The second Scripture speaks to the responsibility we must take for our own decisions so we can stand or fall on whatever we believe God to be saying to us. **Romans 14:22 (NLT2)**

22 You may believe there's nothing wrong with what you are doing, but keep it between yourself and God. Blessed are those who don't feel guilty for doing something they have decided is right.

When a person takes a position on a matter like this, he must understand that whatever decision he/she takes cannot be doctrine. It is their conviction, and they will be answerable to God as to whether they were fully persuaded or did it with a doubtful mind. **Romans 14:23 (NLT2)**

23 But if you have doubts about whether or not you should eat something, you are sinning if you go ahead and do it. For you are not following your convictions. If you do anything you believe is not right, you are sinning.

Surrogate Motherhood

I know quite a few couples that have had babies through surrogate motherhood using the sperm and egg belonging to the couple. It is also possible that some may have used donor egg or sperm. I have heard it said by some preachers that Mary was a surrogate mother because heaven borrowed her womb to cause the Living Word to become human as revealed in **John 1:14 (NLT2)**

14 So the Word became human and made his home among us. He was full of unfailing love and faithfulness. And we have seen his glory, the glory of the Father's one and only Son.

I know for sure that not everybody will agree with this. It boils down to the individual and his or her convictions before the LORD.

Contending with Sickle Cell Disease

Sickle cell disease is not alone in this. There are other genetic disorders that science is addressing to eliminate the problem. Quite a few Churches have gone ahead to rule that two people who are both carriers of the sickle cell gene should not marry no matter how they feel about each other because of the 25% risk of giving birth to a child with sickle cell disease. Those who see the great suffering and misery of children with sickle cell disease agree that such a preventive measure is necessary. But not everybody will agree with the ruling because of the power of faith in God. It is however gratifying to note that technology has advanced to the stage that it can detect the existence of the sickle cell state after fertilization. Because Christians believe that life begins at conception, quite a few may have serious difficulties with this if fertilized eggs or embryos with the double sickling gene are made not to progress by design. The hope is that this technology will continue to advance to detect the presence of the sickling gene in either the sperm or the ovum before fertilization. This advance will make it easier for those who need help to make the decision.

Something that Jacob Knew?

I have always wondered if Jacob knew something we don't know about reproductive biology. He had two wives and two concubines, and from the four of them, he sired 12 boys and one girl. Many understand having same-sex children from a single woman, but having same-sex children from four different women beats probability laws. If Jacob didn't use anything to experience this, then it must be purely divine, to establish God's covenant with Abraham. But we know that Jacob was in the habit of trying to help God out in many things. He took the birthright blessings from Esau by design even though there was a prophecy that the older would serve the younger (Genesis 25:3). Later he tinkered with animal reproduction by affecting their phenotypical appearance to collect his wages from Laban, his father-in-law. The story is quite intriguing.

37 Jacob then took branches of fresh poplar, almond, and plane wood, and peeled the bark, exposing white stripes on the branches.

38 He set the peeled branches in the troughs in front of the sheep — in the water channels where the sheep came to drink. And the sheep bred when they came to drink.

39 The flocks bred in front of the branches and bore streaked, speckled, and spotted young.

40 Jacob separated the lambs and made the flocks face the streaked sheep and the completely dark sheep in Laban's flocks. Then he set his own stock apart and didn't put them with Laban's sheep.

41 Whenever the stronger of the flock were breeding, Jacob placed the branches in the troughs, in full view of the flocks, and they would breed in front of the branches.

42 As for the weaklings of the flocks, he did not put out the branches. So it turned out that the weak sheep belonged to Laban and the stronger ones to Jacob.

43 And the man became very rich. He had many flocks, female and male slaves, and camels and donkeys.

–Genesis 30:37-43 (CSBBible)

I have known families with many children of one gender because they were trying to have the gender they are missing. I was in our Foursquare camp at the convention some years back when a gentleman approached me as a doctor to plead with his wife to stop. She had had nine daughters and was determined to go on until she added at least one son. The gentleman told me that he did not have the financial resources to raise so many children as a worker on minimum wage. But the wife was adamant. She said she was determined to go on until she had a son.

Fortunately, today gender selection is now available through in-vitro fertilization for those who need to balance the gender of their children. Again, they can take recourse to the Scripture repeated here for easy reference: **Romans 14:22 (NLT2)** 22 "You may believe there's nothing wrong with what you are doing, but keep it between yourself and God. Blessed are those who don't feel guilty for doing something they have decided is right." When you decide that gender selection is ok for you in your family, then do it and keep it to yourself. It is between you and God. There are no moral questions involved here that I can see. It may be more a question of faith.

Summary

It is essential to state that the issues I have discussed above do not in any way alter the family structure and the family set-up as taught in the Word of God. Here we see it set out in **Ephesians 6:1-3 (CSBBible)**

1 Children, obey your parents in the Lord, because this is right.

2 Honor your father and mother, which is the first commandment with a promise,

3 so that it may go well with you and that you may have a long life in the land.

In a family, we have a father, a mother, and a child or children. For this reason, I see no place for **single parents by choice** through artificial insemination. Such a scenario will not comply with the Biblical family, with father, mother, and child.

But we have single parents in Church who became single parents due to having children outside wedlock. The Church encourages young ladies who become pregnant outside marriage not to abort the children. The most classic case I have seen is a young lady who became pregnant outside wedlock and went ahead to have the baby. The young man who sired the child was reluctant initially to marry her. After a long period of 10 years or thereabouts, he had a rethink and came back and married her. The boy was close to teenage age when this happened, and now, they are poised to live happily ever after.

We must also recognize those who became widows or widowers and, as a result, become single parents. Most of these scenarios pose significant challenges for which the Holy Spirit supplies grace in abundance.

12

BONE OF MY BONES AND FLESH OF MY FLESH

The Bible records in the Book of Genesis chapter 2, verse 23, that when the Almighty God presented Adam with his wife, he was so delighted that he loudly declared: 'This is now bone of my bones and flesh of my flesh: she shall be called Woman because she was taken from Man."

After this exciting expression of delight at the new development, the Bible declared, "Therefore shall a man leave his father and mother, and shall cleave unto his wife: and they shall be one flesh." In this, the Bible told the man of the constraints that this development would impose on the nuclear family.

The LORD God implied that the husband and wife must constitute the nuclear family to the total exclusion of other members of the extended family. This in no way suggests that they should not have a warm and loving relationship with the other members of their extended family. But it does make it quite clear that a couple must define the boundaries of that extended extra-nuclear family relationship and ensure that it is not a cause of any disruption.

Many of the questions dealt with in the previous chapter, concerning divorce, polygamy, and the like derive from some existing confusion about the nuclear family's imperative demands. Some men fail to cut this lingering umbilical string with their families, so they often rush home to tell everybody what is going on in their home. By doing this, they demonstrate the leadership failure outlined earlier, thereby causing members of their extended family to interfere in their marriage in an entirely unhealthy way.

There is nothing wrong with seeking advice and counsel on the principles of God's word relating to problem areas in one's marriage. What is unhealthy is the demonstration of leadership failure or inability to take charge on Christ's behalf.

To truly appreciate the expression bone of my bones and flesh of my flesh, a man needs to come into the marriage with an overwhelming conviction that he is in God's will in the choice of his marriage partner. He must believe that there will be grace to ensure happiness and peace for his family no matter what life may bring their way because God led him. Such a person would be prepared to do all that the Bible expects of him and more to ensure the union's success. This confident attitude is the way it should be.

However, we may describe people as romanticists who have not appreciated that to produce peace, happiness and stability within the family, you need the interplay of faith and work. Some pray a great deal about their marriage but refuse to accept the changes prescribed by God's word. Quite a few speak a lot about how much peace and harmony require a lot of hard work but do not have the humility to do anything to achieve it.

A man or woman may make a choice that is in the will of God. But whether that marriage attains to its highest potential depends a great deal on the two people involved and how careful they are in obeying the Lord in the areas outlined in this book and other principles in God's word.

Some of us may be enjoying our marriage. Some of us may be enduring ours, sometimes feeling somewhat trapped in there, because of the constraints of the Gospel of the Kingdom of God.

We can have the marriage we desire if we are willing to pay the price of intercession and obedience to the principles in God's word concerning marriage, some of which we reviewed in this book. Those who are unwilling to do this should be prepared to limp along with grace and grit. It is their choice.

However, they should pray that if for reasons of their failings, they cannot have an exciting marital experience, the purposes of God in bringing them together must not fail by any chance. They must consistently pray that whatever pertains to eternity in their union must be preserved.

We need to know that bone of my bones and flesh of my flesh is more than the way I feel about my spouse at any time, whether with joy or sadness. The bone of my bones and flesh of my flesh is not just about how we feel about our union in time; it is also about bringing God glory through our lives together.

A couple must determine to make the very best of their marriage. To love each other dearly and respect each other must be something both husband and wife desire and cherish. They must endeavor to continue to be friends even years after their union. They must choose to maintain an unbroken line of communication no matter the stress they are going through. They must try as much as possible to be open to each other, and never forget to be faithful to their marriage vows whenever they are apart. All these pose significant personal challenges, and sometimes the devil has been known to exploit inherent weaknesses in the individual to destabilize a marriage.

One secret I have found enduringly useful is always relying on the Lord for help in all situations. Those who trust their experience and maturity as Christians may be surprised to find that circumstances can suddenly make an impregnable relationship vulnerable. Relying on the Lord will help us notice when the spirit is pointing to areas of the relationship that are being neglected and call for urgent action. Let us remember that: "To love and to hold till death do us part" can only hold for those in love when they married and who have learned to love by the Holy Spirit's help through the years.

PUTTING IT TOGETHER

How can we summarise all that we have shared in this book? I believe there is no better way than our Lord Jesus Christ's response to a similar question:

[36] Master, which is the great commandment in the law? [37] Jesus said unto him, Thou shalt love the Lord thy God with all thy heart, and with all thy soul, and with all thy mind. [38] This is the first and great commandment. [39] And the second is like unto it, Thou shalt love thy neighbour as thyself.

—Matthew 22:36-38

Success in marriage hinges on the twin question of love for God first and love for our neighbor. The immediate neighbor in marriage is the spouse, followed by the child or children.

I believe one enduring secret to success in love is to first offer our love entirely to God, just like He asked us to do. When we first present all our love to God, the Spirit of God will remove all the unwholesome attributes that we carry in life, which will diminish our love's quality.

The way to do this is to continually offer our love to God in prayer and ask the Holy Spirit to show us how to make our love as pure as God's love. If we are sincere and obedient, the Spirit of God will daily show up the bad patches in our love, like selfishness, greed, inconsistencies, dishonesty, and the like, when they occur and will give us the grace to make changes. He will also teach us the discipline of love and avoid confusing love with indulgence, particularly with our children. This process, conducted through the Holy Spirit's communion, is continuous as we daily meditate on God's word and interact with others. As the Lord purifies our love, we become more and more sensitive to our spouses' needs, striving to give them our best while working to bring out the best in them for our enjoyment and satisfaction. This approach is how we come to learn that in marriage, as in other relationships in life, we reap what we sow. (Galatians 6:7).

EPILOGUE

A book like this is bound to evoke some controversy in the mind of the reader. This response is not surprising because of the various forays into what hitherto might have been unexplored Christian family-life areas.

However and quite categorically, too, one must say that what is intended here is to synthesize God's mind as revealed in God's word concerning the various areas touched to streamline Christian behavior.

The need to streamline Christian behavior was behind our Lord Jesus Christ's advice to the Jews who believed in Him in the Gospel of John, chapter 8, verses 31 and 32.

...If ye continue in My word, then are ye My disciples indeed;

And ye shall know the truth, and the truth shall make you free.

He said the same thing in chapter 13, verses 13 to 17, where He emphasized that practical demonstrations of Christianity were just as crucial as the precepts.

It is noteworthy that the disciples were called Christians first in Antioch, and this was after Barnabas and Saul spent one whole year teaching and streamlining the Christian conduct of the people as noted in Acts 11, verses 25 and 26.

Then departed Barnabas to Tarsus, for to seek Saul:

And when he had found him, he brought him unto Antioch. And it came to pass, that a whole year they assembled themselves with the Church, and taught many people. And the disciples were called Christians first in Antioch.

What happened after this was that the Christian became distinguishable from the non-Christian in society. This emergent distinction is a continuous process from generation to generation as revealed in Ephesians 4:11-15:

And He gave some, apostles; and some prophets; and some, pastors and teachers;

For the perfecting of the saints, for the work of the ministry, for the edifying of the body of Christ:

Till we all come in the unity of the faith, and of the knowledge of the Son of God, unto a perfect man, unto the measure of the stature of the fullness of Christ:

That we henceforth be no more children, tossed to and fro, and carried about with every wind of doctrine, by the sleight of men, and cunning craftiness, whereby they lie in wait to deceive;

But speaking the truth in love, MAY GROW UP INTO HIM IN ALL THINGS, which is the head, even Christ.

Growing up in Him in all things is no mean task, and the Church must continue to seek God's mind in every area.

This book is written from a fellow pilgrim's point of view with a burden that we all ought to walk as the Lord expects us to. As ministers of the gospel, we have a responsibility to continue searching for a more in-depth and better understanding of God's mind in every area of life.

The search is for truth. It is possible that what we have come to see and accept as the truth in God's word concerning any particular issue will revolutionize our lives in that area, causing the inevitable ripples and waves and changes.

When we combine knowledge of the truth with the anointing of the Holy Spirit, we position ourselves to enjoy abundant life in our homes as promised by our Lord. The Word of God is the truth that sets men and women free to serve the Almighty God and His Son Jesus Christ and enjoy a fulfilling life.

But one must not underestimate the burden or burdens that the discovery of truth can place on the individual. Sometimes, it goes beyond burden to real agony of soul that produces real-life dilemmas as the Holy Spirit uses the truth so discovered to wrench the individual away from error and the negative spiritual influence arising from there. The result is greater conformity to the image of God's Son, Jesus Christ, and so, a higher capacity to wield the power of God. I believe the Apostle Paul had this in mind in his second letter to the Corinthians, chapter 10, verses 4 to 6, where he reminded them that:

The weapons of our warfare are not carnal but mighty through God to the pulling down of strongholds; casting down imaginations, and every high thing that exalteth itself against the knowledge of God, and bringing into captivity every thought to the obedience of Christ;

And having in a readiness to revenge all disobedience, when your obedience is fulfilled.

The implication is that one must not expect to use the authority and power deriving from God's word to subdue the devil and his agents when the same word does not rule one's life. In other words, you can only revenge all disobedience by the devil and his agents when your obedience of God's word as revealed to and adequately understood by you, is fulfilled.

Indeed, I know the burdens that truth can impose, the dilemmas it can create, and the upheavals that may result. I have watched these in many lives and have seen people labor and strive to rationalize truth to escape the consequences of its discovery.

I know the unease that follows the rationalization of truth, the emptiness and feeling of powerlessness that follow when we escape from its control, and the fear of the consequences that accompany our rejection.

All these, as unfavorable as they may seem, tell us rather clearly that we belong to Him and that His Holy Spirit is brooding over us so that the Christ nature will form in us. "*My little children, of whom I travail in birth again until Christ be formed in you*" (Galatians 4:19). Those who do not genuinely belong may dispense with truth, ignore its demands, and claim to feel no pressure within. If indeed they sense no pressure within, then it is proof that they do not belong.

For whom the Lord loveth He chasteneth, and scourgeth every son whom He receiveth.

But if ye be without chastisement, whereof all are partakers, then are ye bastards and not sons
—Hebrews 12:6 & 8

Thus, the truth may create pain and hurt, deep anger and disgust, and even fear of the future. But when all the dust has settled, what will remain will be the sweet smell of victory. This victory speaks of the dethronement of self and the uplifting of godly biblical standards that make for peace and harmony. The Spirit of God, working through the human spirit and soul, has successfully enforced conformity with Christ's image. While He was here on earth, our Lord Jesus subjugated His will to that of Almighty God. This subjugation is what shows that eternity and God's will is manifesting through us in time. And we are fully persuaded that what the Almighty God thinks of us is what counts in the end.

It is vital to bear in mind that truth neither creates victors nor vanquished on any issue. Truth serves to ensure freedom from ignorance and conformity to the image of Christ in our lives. There is, therefore, nothing to boast about or gloat over.

Besides, we must also note that truth has a way of drawing from the resources of Almighty God to redress the upheavals that follow its discovery and acceptance by the individual.

This impact is the one fact that encourages the individual to take a stand with truth braving all the odds. The psalmist captured this in Psalm 126 verse 6, where he said:

He that goeth forth and weepeth, bearing precious seed, shall doubtless come again with rejoicing, bringing his sheaves with him.

Anyone of us that faces the challenges of accepting and obeying the truth in any area of our lives must draw inspiration from Hebrews chapter 12 verses 2 to 4, where it says:

We do this by keeping our eyes on Jesus, on whom our faith depends from start to finish. He was willing to die a shameful death on the cross because of the joy he knew would be his afterward. Now He is seated in the place of highest honor beside God's throne in heaven.

Think about all He endured when sinful people did such terrible things to Him so that you don't become weary and give up.

After all, you have not yet given your lives in your struggle against sin. (NLT)